Intellectual Property Law in Serbia

Intellectual Property Law in Serbia

Dušan V. Popović

This book was originally published as a monograph in the International Encyclopaedia of Laws/Intellectual Property Law.

Founding Editor: Roger Blanpain
General Editor: Frank Hendrickx
Volume Editor: Hendrik Vanhees

Wolters Kluwer

Published by:
Kluwer Law International B.V.
PO Box 316
2400 AH Alphen aan den Rijn
The Netherlands
E-mail: international-sales@wolterskluwer.com
Website: www.wolterskluwer.com/en/solutions/kluwerlawinternational

Sold and distributed by:
Wolters Kluwer Legal & Regulatory U.S.
7201 McKinney Circle
Frederick, MD 21704
United States of America
E-mail: customer.service@wolterskluwer.com

ISBN 978-94-035-4255-3

e-Book: ISBN 978-94-035-4260-7
web-PDF: ISBN 978-94-035-4261-4

The Author

Prof. Dr Dušan V. Popović was born in 1978 in Belgrade, Serbia. He is Professor at the Faculty of Law of the University of Belgrade (Serbia), where he teaches Intellectual Property Law, Competition Law and Internet Law. He graduated from the Faculty of Law of the University of Belgrade in 2001. He completed his postgraduate studies in EU Law (*diplôme d'études approfondies*) in 2003 at the University of Nancy (France) and his doctoral studies in Competition Law in 2007 at the University Paris Nanterre (France). He defended his PhD thesis entitled 'Droit communautaire de la concurrence et communications électroniques' with honours (*mention très honorable avec les félicitations du jury à l'unanimité*). He regularly publishes scientific papers in Serbian, French and English. He has received grants from the French Government, the Serbian Government and the Max Planck Institute for Innovation and Competition, enabling him to conduct research on different IP law-related issues. He was the national coordinator of the Tempus project 'Joint Regional Master of Intellectual Property Law', funded by the European Commission and supported by the WIPO Academy. Professor Dušan V. Popović drafted the Serbian Innovation Policy Act (2015) and the Rules on resolution of *.rs* domain name disputes (2010), as well as the amendments to the Serbian Patent Act (2015), Serbian Trademark Act (2015) and the Serbian Copyright Act (2011). He was among EU law specialists who drafted the National Strategy for the Accession of Serbia to the European Union (2005). He serves as the president of the Serbian Domain Name Dispute Resolution Institution, which acts within the auspices of the Serbian Chamber of Commerce. He acted as arbitrator (under the Rules of the Permanent Court of Arbitration, attached to the Serbian Chamber of Commerce) and counsel in arbitration (under LCIA Arbitration Rules, Swiss Rules of International Arbitration and ICSID rules).

The Author

Table of Contents

List of Abbreviations

Art.	Article
Ch.	Chapter
DO	Designation of Origin
EPO	European Patent Organization
GI	Geographical Indication
IP Office	Intellectual Property Office
p.	Page
PCT	Patent Cooperation Treaty
RS	Republic of Serbia
SPC	Supplementary Protection Certificate
UPOV	The International Union for the Protection of New Varieties of Plants
vol.	Volume
WIPO	World Intellectual Property Organization
WTO	World Trade Organization

List of Abbreviations

Preface

This monograph deals with the national legal framework for the protection of intellectual property in the Republic of Serbia (RS). The international intellectual property conventions are not examined in this study, although they are part of Serbian law. Rather, the monograph will focus on Serbian national rules, which are harmonized with the sources of international intellectual property law. The RS is currently engaged in the process of membership negotiations with the World Trade Organization. Therefore, its national IP law is also being influenced by the TRIPS Agreement. Finally, since the RS is an EU candidate country, its intellectual property law is harmonized with the sources of European Union Law to a great extent.

General Introduction

§1. General Background

I. Geography

1. The Republic of Serbia (RS) is situated at the crossroads between Central and Southeast Europe, covering the parts of the Pannonian Plain and the central Balkans. Serbia borders Hungary to the north, Romania and Bulgaria to the east, Macedonia and Albania to the south, and Croatia, Bosnia-Herzegovina and Montenegro to the west. The length of Serbia's border is 2,364 km. The northern portion of the country belongs to central Europe, but in terms of geography and climate, Serbia is also partly a Mediterranean country. The country is landlocked but the Danube, the Europe's second-longest river, connects it with the various European states and the Black Sea. The agricultural regions of Srem, Banat and Bačka, situated in the north of the country, form the province of Vojvodina. The central part of the country, called Šumadija, is characterized by mountains rich in canyons, caves and gorges, as well as well-preserved forests. Kosovo and Metohija, Serbia's southern province, which special status is regulated under the UN Security Council Resolution 1244, is rich in coal.

The lowest spots in the country are the Danube and Timok rivers (35 metres), while the highest point is the mountain Midzor (2,169 metres). The territory of Serbia is the shortest link between Western Europe and the Middle East. Manny international roads and railway lines run through the country's river valleys. The country's territory occupies an area of 88,407 square kilometres. Serbian rivers belong to the basins of the Adriatic, Black and Aegean Seas. Three rivers are navigable – the Danube, Sava and Tisa. The longest river is the Danube, which flows for 588 km through the country. There are several mountain ranges in Serbia: Dinaric Alps in the west, Rhodope mountain in the south, Carpathian and Balkan mountains in the east, separated by a group of dome mountains along the Morava river valley. Serbia is in the Central European Time zone. Its climate is temperate continental, with a gradual transition between the four seasons of the year.

II. Cultural Composition

2. The cultural composition of Serbia is quite diverse, which is a consequence of the country's very turbulent past. The majority of population is composed of Serbs, and they represent around 83% of the country's 7.2 million citizens (Kosovo and Metohija excluded). There are other thirty-seven ethnicities living in Serbia, the largest groups among them being the Hungarian minority (3.5%), the Romany minority (2.1%) and the Bosniak minority (2%). The feeling of national identity of minorities living in Serbia is rather strong. The largest minority communities live in the northern province of Vojvodina (Hungarians, Slovaks, Rusyns and others) and in the region of Raška (Bosniaks – Muslim minority).

3. Serbia is predominantly a Christian country. Serbs are Orthodox Christians, while there are other religions among the minorities (Catholics, Protestants, Muslims etc.). The official language is Serbian. The members of the minority communities may use their languages in administrative and educational institutions. In the northern province of Vojvodina, Hungarian, Slovak, Romanian, Croatian and Rusyn are recognized as official languages, further to Serbian.

4. The illiteracy rate is about 2% of population aged 15 and above. In Serbia, around 11% of population pursued higher (university) education.

III. Political System

5. Throughout its turbulent history, Serbia has been both a kingdom and a republic. It existed as an independent country, survived the occupation by the Ottoman Empire, formed and joined Yugoslavia, and became independent once the process of dissolution of Yugoslavia was over. At present, Serbia is an independent country, with a democratic republican political system. The present Constitution, dating from 2006, defines the RS as a state of Serbian people and all citizens who live in it. The country is based on the rule of law and social justice, principles of civil democracy, human and minority rights and freedoms, and commitment to European principles and values. Human and minority rights guaranteed by the Constitution are implemented directly. The sovereignty is vested in citizens who exercise it through referendums, people's initiatives and freely elected representatives. It is also proclaimed that no state body, political organization, group or individual may usurp the sovereignty from the citizens, or establish government against the freely expressed will of the citizens.

6. The Constitution of the RS proclaims the rule of law as one of the founding principles of the country's political system. The rule of law is exercised through free and direct elections, constitutional guarantees of human and minority rights, separation of power, independent judiciary and observance of Constitution and law by the authorities. The political system is based on the division of power into legislative power, executive power and judiciary. The relation between the three branches of power is based on the principles of mutual control and balance. The Constitution particularly emphasizes the independence of the judiciary power. State power is restricted by the right of citizens to provincial autonomy and local self-government.

The Constitution defines the RS as a secular state. No religion may be established as state or mandatory religion. Churches and religious communities must be separated from the state. The state guarantees the equality of women and men and the development of equal opportunity policy. Other forms of discrimination are equally prohibited, in particular discrimination based on race, national origin, social origin, birth, religion, political or other opinion, property status, culture, language, age, or mental or physical disability.

7. Further to the central government and local self-government units, the political power is exercised by autonomous provinces of Vojvodina, in the north of the country, and Kosovo and Metohija, in the south. The provinces are competent in the field of urban planning, agriculture, forestry, transport, education, sport, culture and social welfare. Their supreme body is the Assembly, which elects the Provincial Government. Provinces enjoy financial autonomy. The province of Kosovo and Metohija enjoys a special status, following the 1999 conflict and the adoption of the 2006 Constitution. The province of Kosovo declared its independence from Serbia in 2008, which is not recognized by the central government in Belgrade.

8. The constitutional and legislative power is vested in the National Assembly (in Serbian, *Narodna skupština*). The National Assembly is the supreme representative body, which consists of 250 deputies, elected on direct elections by secret ballot. Members of the parliament are elected in the RS as one electoral unit, by use of proportional electoral system. Only election lists that received a minimum of 3% of votes of the total number of voters who had voted are allowed to participate in the distribution of deputies' mandates. However, the exception is made with respect to political parties of national minorities, which are allowed to participate in the distribution of mandates regardless of the number of votes they received. The members of the parliament enjoy immunity and they may not accept criminal or other liability for the expressed opinion or the cast vote in performing their public function. The Assembly adopts decision by majority vote of deputies at the session at which the majority of deputies are present. Certain decisions are adopted by means of majority vote of all deputies of the National Assembly. That is the case *inter alia* with a decision to elect judges of the Constitutional Court, to elect and dismiss the governor of the National Bank, to elect judges and public prosecutors, or to adopt the budget. The National Assembly is convoked for two regular sessions per year. Extraordinary sessions may also be convoked. A right to propose laws, other regulations and general acts belongs to every deputy, the Government, assemblies of autonomous provinces or minimum of 30,000 voters.

9. The executive power is exercised by the Government of the RS. The Government establishes and pursues public policies, executes laws and other general acts of the National Assembly, adopts by-laws, proposes laws and other general acts to the National Assembly, directs the work of public administration bodies and supervises their work. The Government is accountable to the National Assembly of the RS. The Government consists of the Prime Minister, one or more Vice-Presidents and ministers. A candidate for the Prime Minister is proposed to the National Assembly by the president of the Republic, after he/she considers the opinions of representatives of elected election lists. The candidate for the Prime Minister presents to the National Assembly the Government's Programme and proposes its constitution. The National Assembly simultaneously votes on the Government's Programme and the election of the Prime Minister and members of the Government.

10. Judicial power in the RS belongs to the courts of general and special jurisdiction. The Supreme Court of Cassation is the Supreme Court in the RS. Its seat is in Belgrade. The judicial system includes basic courts (in Serbian, *Osnovni sud*), higher courts (in Serbian, *Viši sud*), appellate courts (in Serbian, *Apelacioni sud*), commercial courts (in Serbian, *Privredni sud*), appellate commercial courts (in Serbian, *Privredni apelacioni sud*), misdemeanour courts (in Serbian, *Prekršajni sud*), misdemeanour appellate court (in Serbian, *Prekršajni apelacioni sud*) and the Administrative Court (in Serbian, *Upravni sud*). Judges have a permanent tenure. Exceptionally, a person who is elected a judge for the first time is appointed for a period of three years. The judges are elected on proposal of the High Judicial Council by the National Assembly for a period of three years. Following that period, a judge is being elected to a permanent tenure by the High Judicial Council. The High Judicial Council is an autonomous body vested with guaranteeing the independence of courts and judges from other branches of law. The members of the Council are the president of the Supreme Court of Cassation, the minister of justice and the president of the Judicial Committee of the National Assembly, as the members ex officio, as well as eight members elected by the National Assembly among the judges and prominent lawyers.

The Constitutional Court of the RS (in Serbian, *Ustavni sud*) enjoys special status with respect to both its competences and the manner in which its judges are appointed. The Constitutional Court decides on compliance of laws and other general acts with the Constitution, generally accepted rules of the international law and ratified international treaties. It also decides on compliance of ratified international treaties with the Constitution, compliance of other general acts with the law, compliances of Statute and other general acts of autonomous provinces and self-government units with the Constitution and the Law. The Constitutional Court is also competent for electoral disputes, as well as for the conflict of jurisdiction disputes. The Court has fifteen justices who are appointed for a period of nine years. Five justices are appointed by the National Assembly, another five by the president of the Republic, and another five at the general session of the Supreme Court of Cassation.

11. The president of the Republic represents the state unity of the RS. The president is in charge of representing the country internally and abroad, promulgating laws upon his decree, proposing to the National Assembly a candidate for the Prime Minister, appointing and dismissing, upon his decree, ambassadors, upon the proposal of the Government, grant amnesties and award honours. The president of the Republic is elected in direct elections, by secret ballot. The president of the Republic may not perform another public function or professional duty. The term of office of the president of the Republic lasts five years and begins from the day of taking the oath before the National Assembly.

12. The 2006 Constitution of the RS introduced the institution of the Civic Defender/Ombudsman (in Serbian, *Zaštitnik građana*), as an independent state body in charge of protecting the citizens' rights and monitoring the work of public administration bodies, bodies in charge of legal protection of proprietary rights and interests of the RS, and other bodies and organizations to which public powers have been delegated. The Civic Defender is elected and dismissed by the National Assembly, to which he/she accounts for his/her work. The Civic Defender enjoys immunity identical to the one enjoyed by the deputies. The Civic Defender is not however authorized to monitor the work of the National Assembly, president of the Republic, Government, Constitutional Court, other courts and the Public Prosecutor's Offices.

13. The present political life in Serbia is dominated by two political parties – the Serbian Progressive Party (in Serbian, *Srpska napredna stranka*) and by the Democratic Party (in Serbian, *Demokratska stranka*). The Serbian Progressive Party is a centre-right, conservative political party. It was formed in 2008 when the group of influential members left the Serbian Radical Party. The Democratic Party is a centre-left, social-democratic and social-liberal political party. The party was founded in 1990 by a group of Serbian intellectuals as a revival of the Democratic Party that existed in the Kingdom of Yugoslavia. The Democratic Party is a member of the Socialist International, the Progressive Alliance and an associate member of the Party of European Socialists. Since the law does not prohibit pre-electoral coalitions, numerous other minor parties also enter the parliament.

IV. Population Statistics

14. The population of Serbia is approximately 7.2 million inhabitants (Kosovo and Metohija excluded). The capital city of Belgrade has around 1.7 million citizens. The second-largest city is the capital of the Province of Vojvodina, Novi Sad, with around 336,000 inhabitants. The overall population density is medium as it stands at 92.8 inhabitants per square kilometre. Approximately 55% of the population lives in urban areas. Serbia has a comparatively old overall population. Approximately 42% of the population is aged 25–54 years. Median age of population is 41.9 years, being slightly lower for male population – 40.2 years and higher for female population – 43.6 years. The population growth rate is negative and it stands at minus 0.46%. The birth rate is 9.08 births per 1000 inhabitants, while the death rate is 13.66 deaths per 1000 inhabitants (2015 estimation).

§2. Historical Background

15. The territory of Serbia has been inhabited since 40,000 BC when the first settlements were made. The Celtic tribe of Scordisci settled in the area in the third century BC and built their capital city Singidunum (at present, Belgrade). The Romans conquered the territory in the second century BC. In the third and fourth centuries, several Roman emperors were born on the soil of modern Serbia – Aurelian, Probus, Galerius and Constantine the Great. In the fourth century, Sirmium (*Sremska Mitrovica* at present) was one of the capitals of the Roman Empire. After the Roman Empire divided, the territory of Serbia became part of its Eastern portion – the Byzantine.

16. In the sixth century, Slavic tribes from the Danube Basin started settling in the Balkans. Serbs in the East Roman (Byzantine) world lived in the 'Slav lands', territories which were initially out of Byzantine control. The first Serbian Principality of Vlastimirovići was established in the eighth century. Christianity was accepted as a state religion in 870. The Principality of Vlastimirovići evolved into a Grand Principality by the eleventh century. In 1166, Stefan Nemanja assumed the throne, which marked the establishment of the Nemanjić dynasty. Nemanja's son Rastko Nemanjić (1174–1236) strongly contributed to the development of the Serbian state and church. He authored the first 'constitutional' rules (in ancient Serbian, *Zakonopravilo*) and gained autocephaly for the Serbian Church in 1217. He was the first archbishop of the Serbian Church, and he is considered the founder of the Serbian Orthodox Church. Rastko Nemanjić founded schools and hospitals; therefore, he is also considered the founder of the Serbian educational and medical system. The Serbian Orthodox Church canonized him as Saint Sava. In modern Serbia, the Saint Sava's Day, the 27th of January, is celebrated as the Day of schools and other educational institutions. Numerous celebrations are organized every year with a view of preserving the memory of Saint Sava. Sava's brother Stefan Nemanjić – Stefan the First Crowned established the Serbian Kingdom in 1217. Stefan Nemanjić is considered one of the most successful Serbian medieval rulers. The Dynasty Nemanjić was very successful in expanding the territory of Serbia which became one of the most powerful European states at the time. It spread over the territories of modern Serbia, Bosnia, Montenegro, Macedonia, Bulgaria, Albania and Greece. In 1346, Dušan the Mighty, another significant member of the Nemanjić Dynasty, established the Serbian Empire.

17. The independent Serbian state disappeared by the mid-sixteenth century, torn by Ottoman conquest. The Ottoman occupation, which lasted for several centuries, is considered as one of the most difficult periods in the Serbian history. A series of uprisings between 1804 and 1835 resulted in the gradual regaining of independence from the Ottomans. The second uprising in 1815, under the leadership of Miloš Obrenović, resulted in the establishment of the Principality recognized by the Ottoman Empire. The right to hereditary rule was also recognized which led to the establishment of the new Serbian Dynasty Obrenović (1815–1903, except between 1842–1858). The first written Constitution was adopted on 15 February 1835. In modern Serbia, that day is celebrated as the Serbian National Day. The independence of Serbia was fully recognized by the 'Great Powers' in the Berlin Congress of 1878.

In 1903, the reign of the Dynasty Obrenović was ended by the assassination of the king Aleksandar I Obrenović in the event known as 'May Overthrow'. The Dynasty Karadjordjević took over and ruled until the beginning of World War II. At the beginning of the twentieth century, Serbia successfully participated in the Balkan wars. The First Balkan War (1912–1913) was led by Serbia, Montenegro, Greece and Bulgaria against the Ottoman Empire, while the Second Balkan War (1913) was led by Bulgaria against Serbia and Greece. Following these wars, Serbia significantly expanded its territory by regaining the territory of 'Old Serbia' (parts of Macedonia, Kosovo and Raška). The assassination of Austrian Crown Prince Franz Ferdinand in the Bosnian capital Sarajevo by a Bosnian Serb Gavrilo Princip served as a pretext for the Austrian declaration of war on Serbia on 28 June 1914. This event marked the beginning of World War I (1914–1918). Austria occupied Serbia but this did not prevent the forming of the Serbian Army in Exile. Supported by the allies, the Serbian Army liberated the country in 1918. The end of World War I and the collapse of the Austro-Hungarian and Ottoman Empires facilitated the proclaiming of the Kingdom of Serbs, Croats and Slovenes in December 1918. This state, renamed in 1929 into the Kingdom of Yugoslavia, was ruled by the Serbian Dynasty Karadjordjević.

18. In 1941, the Kingdom of Yugoslavia was invaded and occupied by Nazi Germany, Italy, Hungary and Bulgaria. A royal government in exile was established in London. During the occupation, Serbian people joined the resistance movement of Partisans and actively fought the enemy. However, Partisans used the resistance movement to spread their communist/socialist ideas, which resulted in the establishment of the Federal People's Republic of Yugoslavia following the end of World War II in 1945. In 1963, the country was renamed the Socialist Federal Republic of Yugoslavia. The country was organized into six republics and two autonomous provinces. The republics were: Serbia, Croatia, Bosnia and Herzegovina, Montenegro, Macedonia and Slovenia. Both autonomous provinces were formed on the territory of Serbia – Vojvodina, in northern Serbia, and Kosovo and Metohija, in southern Serbia. The country's life-long president Josip Broz Tito died in 1980, which accelerated the political and economic crisis Yugoslavia was experiencing. The 1991 proclamations of independence by Slovenia and Croatia marked the beginning of the civil war which lasted throughout the 1990s.

19. While Slovenia, Croatia, Bosnia and Herzegovina, and Macedonia proclaimed independence, Serbia and Montenegro remained together and formed the Federal Republic of Yugoslavia in 1992. During the last decade of the twentieth century, Serbian president Slobodan Milošević was accused by the Western countries of significantly contributing to the dissolution of Yugoslavia and influencing the wars that spread in other parts of the former federation. The confrontations between Serbian police and Kosovo Albanians led to the 1999 NATO military intervention against FR Yugoslavia. The fall of Milošević in 2000 ended the international isolation of the country. In 2003, FR Yugoslavia was renamed and reconstituted as the State Union of Serbia and Montenegro. Following the proclamation of independence of Montenegro, the National Assembly of Serbia on 5 June 2006 declared Serbia to be the legal successor to the former State Union. This event marks the end of the 'Yugoslav path' Serbia undertook in 1918 by creating the Kingdom of Serbs, Croats and Slovenes.

On 17 February 2008, Serbian southern province of Kosovo declared independence, which is not recognized by Belgrade.

Chapter 1. Copyright and Neighbouring Rights

§1. Sources – Legislation

20. The development of Serbian copyright and neighbouring rights protection system may be traced from the end of the nineteenth century and the beginning of the twentieth century. Copyright was already protected prior to World War I, in parts of Serbia which belonged to the Austrian-Hungarian Empire. However, the development of Serbian copyright and neighbouring rights system *stricto sensu* should be connected with the adoption of the first Copyright Act of the Kingdom of Yugoslavia in 1929. This Act was drafted under the strong influence of the German Copyright Act and was generally harmonized with the Berne Convention, to which the Kingdom of Yugoslavia acceded in 1930.

21. Following World War II, the Kingdom of Yugoslavia was succeeded by the Democratic Federal Yugoslavia (later: Socialist Federative Republic (SFR) of Yugoslavia). The significant social and political changes in the country were followed by the establishment of the new legal system. The first Copyright Act in socialist Yugoslavia was adopted in 1946. This Act was not aligned with the provisions of the Berne Convention, to which the country acceded for the second time in 1951. Further harmonization of the national copyright system with international conventions was achieved through the adoption of subsequent Copyright Acts in 1957, 1968 and 1978. Copyright and neighbouring rights were efficiently protected to an extent which reached beyond the general context of social organization at the time.

22. From 1990 onwards, the copyright and neighbouring rights system experienced rapid progress. The Federal Republic of Yugoslavia, which succeeded to the SFR Yugoslavia, acceded to remaining copyright and neighbouring rights conventions and started harmonizing its national copyright law with the European Union directives and the Agreement on Trade-Related Aspects of Intellectual Property Rights. This was achieved through the adoption of the Copyright and Neighbouring Rights Act in 1998. The rapid harmonization of the Serbian copyright and neighbouring rights system continued with the adoption of the new Copyright and Neighbouring Rights Act in 2004 and the present Act in 2009.

23. Pursuant to the Constitution of the RS,[1] copyright belongs to the category of human rights and freedoms of every man and citizen. Article 73.1 of the Constitution of the RS sets forth that scientific and artistic creativity is unrestricted. Moreover, Article 73.2 sets forth that oral and pecuniary rights are guaranteed to authors of scientific and artistic works, in accordance with the law. Pursuant to the Constitution, the RS shall assist and promote development of science, culture and art. The main legislative source of contemporary copyright law in Serbia is the Copyright and Neighbouring Rights Act, adopted in 2009, and amended in 2011, 2012 and

1. Official Journal of the Republic of Serbia, n° 98/2006.

2019.[2] The Copyright and Neighbouring Rights Act has generally been harmonized with all international treaties, conventions and agreements, which regulate the area of copyright and neighbouring rights,[3] as well as with the majority of EU directives concerning copyright and related rights, which were enacted prior to its adoption. The RS ratified the following international conventions:

- Berne Convention for the Protection of Literary and Artistic Works.[4]
- Universal Copyright Convention as revised at Paris on 24 July 1971.[5]
- Convention Establishing the World Intellectual Property Organization (WIPO).[6]
- Rome Convention for the Protection of Performers, Producers of Phonograms and Broadcasting Organizations.[7]
- Convention for the Protection of Producers of Phonograms Against Unauthorized Duplication of Their Phonograms.[8]
- World Intellectual Property Organization Copyright Treaty.[9]
- World Intellectual Property Organization Performances and Phonograms Treaty.[10]
- Marrakesh Treaty to Facilitate Access to Published Works for Persons Who Are Blind, Visually Impaired or Otherwise Print Disabled.[11]

The Government of the RS adopted the following by-laws to implement the Copyright and Neighbouring Rights Act:

- Regulation on the conditions the deposited copies of copyright-protected works and subject matter of neighbouring rights need to fulfil, on the entry in the register and deposition of copyright-protected works and subject matter of neighbouring rights, and on the contents of the registration of deposited copyright-protected works and subject matter of neighbouring rights with the competent authority.[12]
- Regulation laying down the list of technical devices and audio and visual carriers in relation to which a levy is to be paid to owners of copyright and neighbouring rights.[13]

2. *Ibid.*, n° 104/2009, 99/2011, 119/2012, 29/2016 (decision of the Constitutional Court) and 66/2019.

3. World Intellectual Property Organization Performances and Phonograms Treaty (ratification: Official Journal of the Federal Republic of Yugoslavia – International Treaties n° 13/2002).
4. Official Journal of the Federative Socialist Republic of Yugoslavia – International Treaties, n° 4/1986.
5. *Ibid.*, n° 54/73.
6. *Ibid.*, n° 31/72 and 4/86.
7. Official Journal of the Federal Republic of Yugoslavia – International Treaties, n° 13/2002.
8. *Ibid.*, n° 13/2002.
9. *Ibid.*
10. *Ibid.*
11. Official Journal of the Republic of Serbia n° 1/2020.
12. *Ibid.*, n° 45/2010.
13. *Ibid.*

– Regulation on the manner of keeping electronic records of broadcasting and rebroadcasting of copyright-protected works.[14]

24. Further to the Copyright and Neighbouring Rights Act, the area of copyright and neighbouring rights is regulated by the Act on Special Competencies for Efficient Protection of Intellectual Property Rights.[15] In a broader sense, the Act on Optical Discs also forms part of the Serbian copyright and neighbouring rights system.[16] This Act lays down rules on manufacturing of optical discs, import and export of production parts and equipment used for manufacturing of optical discs, as well as commercial reproduction, export, import and distribution of optical discs.

§2. Subject Matter of Protection

25. Copyright protects the work of an author. The work of an author is an original intellectual creation, expressed in a certain form, regardless of its artistic, scientific or other value, its purpose, size, contents and way of manifestation, as well as the permissibility of public communication of its contents. The works protected by copyright are mentioned by way of example in the Copyright and Neighbouring Rights Act:

– written works (books, brochures, articles, translations, computer programs along with their technical and user documentation in any form of their expression, including their preparatory design material, etc.);
– spoken works (lectures, speeches, orations, etc.);
– dramatic, dramatic-musical, choreographic and pantomime works, as well as works originating from folklore;
– music works, with or without words;
– films (cinematographic and television works);
– fine art works (paintings, drawings, sketches, graphics, sculptures, etc.);
– works of architecture, applied art and industrial design;
– cartographic works (geographic and topographic maps);
– drawings, sketches, dummies and photographs; and
– the direction of a theatre play.[17]

26. Derivative works may also enjoy copyright protection. A derivative work is an intellectual creation in which the characteristic elements of the modified (original) work are recognizable (e.g., music remixes, arrangements, adaptations). The copyright protection of a derivative work does not limit the rights of the author of the modified (original) work.

14. *Ibid.*, nº 108/2014.
15. *Ibid.*, nº 46/2006 and 104/2009.
16. *Ibid.*, nº 52/2011.
17. *See* Copyright and Neighbouring Rights Act, Art. 2.

27. However, certain works are excluded from copyright protection. Copyright protects expressions and not ideas, procedures and methods of operations, or mathematical concepts as such. Copyright does not protect concepts, principles and instructions included in a work either. Finally, the following intellectual creations are also excluded from copyright protection: laws, decrees, regulations, official materials of state bodies, submissions and other documents presented in the administrative or court proceedings.

§3. Conditions of Protection

28. The Copyright and Neighbouring Rights Act prescribes four conditions for copyright protection.[18] First, the copyrighted work may only be the result of intellectual activity of a human being. However, a human being may use technical devices as means of support when creating a work. The work within the meaning of the Copyright and Neighbouring Rights Act may not be a creation that already existed in the nature before being found or presented by a human (e.g., a piece of wood, a stone).

29. Second, the work within the meaning of the copyright rules must comprise certain intellectual/spiritual content. This requirement should be understood as the aptitude of a work to communicate directly with the users. The communication should stem from the contents of the work, without the need to recourse to instructions or explanations which are not comprised by the contents of the work. For example, a credit card is undoubtedly an intellectual creation, but it is not a work within the meaning of Serbian copyright rules, since it is not a means of a direct communication between the users (individuals). The meaning of such an intellectual creation can be understood only by recourse to the instructions which are outside of the intellectual creation itself.

30. Third, the work within the meaning of the Copyright and Neighbouring Rights Act must be expressed in a certain form. The form should not necessarily be understood as a material one, since the Act does not require the work to be expressed in a material/tangible form. In Serbian copyright law, the requirement of form is understood as an aptitude of a work to be expressed through a system of signs/codes which are comprehensible to humans. The codes used to express a certain work may differ: words, colours, shapes, music sounds, etc.

31. The fourth requirement that an intellectual creation must meet to qualify for the copyright protection is the requirement of originality. Only original creations may be qualified as works within the meaning of the Copyright and Neighbouring Rights Act. Originality should be understood as individuality or uniqueness of a certain intellectual creation. This requirement should not be confused with the requirement of novelty, typical for industrial property protection. An intellectual creation is deemed original if the personality of its author is reflected in it. Therefore, an

18. *Ibid.*

intellectual creation is original if it does not represent an imitation of an existing work or does not result from the activity which is strictly determined by external framework not allowing any individuality to be expressed.

§4. Ownership

32. An author is a natural person who has created a work of authorship. A person whose name, pseudonym or sign is stated on copies of the work or is referred to on the occasion of publication of the work shall be considered an author, until proven to the contrary. However, a natural or legal person, the designation or name of which is displayed on the film shall be considered as the producer (not the author) of the work, until proven to the contrary. Besides the author, there may be owners of copyright which acquired it in a derivative manner, in accordance with the law (e.g., a successor in title). If the author is unknown (the work is anonymous or created under pseudonym), the copyright is held by its publisher if the work is published, or by the person who has disclosed it if the work is disclosed but not published. Once the identity of the author is established, the rights of the publisher and/or the person who disclosed the work shall be terminated.

33. Works of authorship may be the fruit of collaboration of two or more persons (in Serbian, *koautorsko delo*).[19] A co-author is a natural person who has created a work of authorship by means of engaging into creative activity with another person(s). Co-authors are joint owners of the copyright, unless otherwise provided by the contract governing their mutual relations. Therefore, the consent of all co-authors is necessary for the exercise of the copyright and its assignment. In exercising its rights, a co-author must act bona fide. A co-author may not withhold its consent contrary to the principle of good faith and fair dealing, or do anything that is harmful or could be harmful to the interests of other co-authors. Each co-author is authorized to file an action for the protection of right with respect to the co-authored work, in which case it acts on its own name and for its own behalf. Co-authors share the economic benefit from exploiting a co-authored work in proportion to the actual contribution made by each of them to the creation of such work, unless otherwise agreed on.

34. The Copyright and Neighbouring Rights Act prescribes a special legal regime of co-authorship of films. In Serbian copyright law, the notion of film comprises both cinematographic and television works. Namely, the scriptwriter, director and chief cameraman are always regarded as co-authors of a film. If music makes up an essential component of a film and it has been composed for that film, then also the composer will be regarded as a co-author. In a cartoon and/or animated film, or in a film where drawings or animation are its essential elements, the main film-animator will also be deemed to be the co-author of the film.

19. *Ibid.*, Arts 10–11.

35. The co-authorship of a work should be distinguished from the act of combining of works (in Serbian, *spojeno delo*). If two or more authors combine their independently created works for the sake of joint exploitation, each author reserves its right on its work. The relations between the authors of combined works are determined by contract. Contrary to co-authored works, creative contributions of each author in a combined work may be separated from each other and exploited independently.

36. If a person has created a work as an employee in the performance of his working duties, the employer is authorized to disclose such work and economically exploit it in the course of its business activities for a period of five years from the completion of the work, unless otherwise provided by the company-level agreement or employment agreement.[20] While the employer exercises pecuniary rights with respect to the work of authorship, the employee has the right to remuneration, the amount of which depends on the economic effects of the work's exploitation. Upon the expiration of the five-year term, the author shall acquire the exclusive pecuniary rights on the work. The owner of moral rights shall be the author of a work (employee). Therefore, when using the work of authorship created by an employee, the employer must always indicate the author's name, pseudonym or sign. The Copyright and Neighbouring Rights Act prescribes a special legal regime for computer programs or a database created by an employee in the performance of its working duties. The pecuniary rights with respect to such works are permanently held by the employer, unless otherwise agreed.

37. Finally, the creation of a work of authorship may be commissioned by a third party. Under a contract of commissioning a work of authorship, the author undertakes to create a work and to hand over its copy to the commissioning party.[21] The commissioning party has the right to make the work available to the public and to market the copy of the work. The author retains other rights with respect to the work, unless otherwise agreed by the parties. The party commissioning a work of authorship has the right to direct and control the production of the work, without substantially restricting the author's freedom of artistic, technical or scientific expression. If the work of authorship in question is a computer programme, the commissioning party shall acquire all rights as to the economic exploitation of the programme, unless otherwise agreed by the parties.

§5. Transfer

38. Given the complex legal nature of copyright and performer's right, the author and the performer cannot assign the exclusive rights with respect to the work of authorship/performance in their entirety. Only one or more pecuniary rights may be assigned to another person. Moral rights cannot be assigned or licensed, since they represent the inherent relation between the creator and its work.

---

20. *Ibid.*, Arts 98–101.
21. *Ibid.*, Arts 95–96.

39. If a copyright is transferred by way of inheritance, the author's heirs may exercise only the 'negative aspects' of moral rights (e.g., the right to oppose unbecoming exploitation of the work). 'Positive' moral rights cannot be exercised (e.g., publishing of undisclosed work, if the author had prohibited it during his lifetime). Further to the heirs, associations of authors, as well as institutions in the field of culture, science and arts may also protect moral rights relating to the recognition of authorship, protection of the integrity of work, or prohibition of unbecoming exploitation of the work. Pecuniary rights are inheritable.

40. The author or his/her successor in rights may license some or all of the pecuniary rights on his/her work. The licensing may be either exclusive or non-exclusive. If a licence is a non-exclusive one, the licensee is not authorized either to prohibit third parties from exploiting the copyrighted work, or to sub-license its right. If there is a doubt as to the character of a licence (i.e., the contract is not clearly stating whether the licence in question is exclusive or non-exclusive), the licensing of pecuniary rights shall be deemed to be non-exclusive. The licensing of pecuniary rights with respect to the work of authorship may be limited in terms of subject matter (one or more pecuniary rights), territory and time. In case of territorial limitation, the licensee is authorized to exploit the work of authorship within a specified territory, which is smaller than the one in which the copyright exists. In the case of temporal limitation, the licensee is authorized to exploit the work of authorship within a specified period, which is shorter than the period of validity of the copyright with respect to such work. The licensing of pecuniary right on a work, which is yet to be created, is allowed on condition that the kind of the work and ways of exploiting it are determined in the licensing agreement. However, any licensing of pecuniary rights on all future works of an author, as well as on still unknown forms of exploiting a work, is null and void.

41. As a *lex specialis*, the Copyright and Neighboring Rights Act lays down certain specific rules on copyright agreements.[22] Copyright agreements must be concluded in written form. A copyright agreement must include the following: names of contracting parties, title and/or identification of the work of authorship, rights that are the subject matter of licensing or cession, amount of remuneration, if any, and the method and terms for its payment, as well as limitations related to content, territory and time, if any. In the event of doubt as to the contents and scope of the rights being licensed or ceded by the copyright contract, it shall be deemed that fewer rights have been licensed or assigned. The licensing and/or cession of a right to exploit a work shall also mean the licence for making such modifications in the work that are technically inevitable or usual for such exploitation of the work. If the profit made by exploiting a work of authorship is evidently disproportionate to the contractual remuneration, the author or his/her heir shall have the right to request the contract to be modified for the purpose of eliminating such disproportion. If the author's remuneration is not agreed upon and if the profit made by the use of the work of an author exceeds the costs of its use, allowing therewith the payment of

22. *Ibid.*, Arts 67–72. Rules on contracts and torts apply as *lex generalis*.

author's remuneration, the author or his/her heir shall have the right to request the contract to be modified by including such remuneration in the contract.

42. The author or his/her heir may withhold the permission granted or revoke a licensed pecuniary right, if the acquirer of permission or licensee is not exercising the acquired right or if the right is exercised to a lesser extent than agreed, whereby jeopardizing the interests of the author or his/her heir. The author or his heir may not withhold the permission granted or revoke a licensed pecuniary right if the acquirer is not exercising the right or is doing so inadequately for reasons for which the author or his/her heir is responsible. Prior to withholding the permission or revoking the right, the author or his/her heir shall notify the acquirer of the permission or right accordingly, providing a reasonable period of time within which the acquirer is to commence exercising the acquired right or doing so to the agreed extent.

43. The author may withhold the permission granted or revoke the licensed pecuniary right, if he/she is of the opinion that the exploitation of the work could be detrimental to his/her creative or personal reputation, for reasons arisen subsequent to the conclusion of the copyright contract, for which the acquirer of the right is not responsible. The author must indemnify the acquirer of the right for the real damage sustained.

44. The Copyright and Neighbouring Rights Act prescribes specific rules with respect to certain types of copyright agreements, such as the publishing contract, contract on performance of a work of authorship, contract on adaptation or alteration of a work of authorship, contract on film production, and contract on commissioning of a work of authorship.

§6. Scope of Exclusive Rights

45. Copyright is a single right which consists of three components: (1) moral rights of an author, which protect the author's personal connections with his/her work; (2) pecuniary or economic rights of an author, which protect the author's economic interests in his/her work; and (3) other rights of an author, which protect other interests of an author in his/her work.

I. Moral Rights

46. The Serbian Copyright and Neighbouring Rights Act provides for the following moral rights of the author:

- the right to claim authorship of the work;
- the right to claim the author's name;
- the right of disclosure;
- the right of protection of the work's integrity; and

– the right to oppose unbecoming exploitation of the work.

The moral rights of an author are not transferable by contract. The author's heirs may exercise all powers with respect to the author's moral rights, except for the right to publish an undisclosed work, if the author has prohibited it, and the right to modify the work. Apart from the author's heirs, associations of authors and institutions in the fields of culture, science and art may also protect the author's rights relating to authorship, integrity of the work and prohibition of unbecoming exploitation of the work. Moral rights last even after the expiration of the author's pecuniary rights.

II. Pecuniary Rights

47. The Copyright and Neighbouring Rights Act states that every author has the right to commercially exploit his/her work, as well as the work resulting from the modification of his/her work.[23] The authors are entitled to remuneration for exploitation of their work by another person, unless otherwise provided by the Copyright and Neighbouring Rights Act or a contract. The Act lays down several economic rights, which correspond to different modalities of use of a work. These are:

– the reproduction right;
– the distribution right;
– the right of rental;
– the right of representation;
– the right to transmit public performance of a work by means of technical devices;
– the right of broadcasting;
– the right of re-broadcasting;
– the right of communication to the public of a work by wire or wireless means, including the making available to the public of a work in an interactive way;
– the right of adaptation;
– the right of public communication of a broadcasted work; and
– the right of public communication of a work fixed in an audio and/or visual medium.

A. The Reproduction Right

48. The reproduction right gives its holder the exclusive right to make one or more copies of its work. The author has the exclusive right to authorize or prohibit fixation or reproduction of his work in its entirety or in part, by any means, in any form, in any manner, permanently or temporarily, directly or indirectly. By means of example, the Copyright and Neighbouring Rights Act enumerates several reproduction techniques: reproduction by graphic procedures, photocopying and other

23. *See,* Copyright and Neighbouring Rights Act, Art. 19.

photographic procedures achieving the same result, sound or visual recording, erecting the work of architecture, storage of the work in electronic form into the memory of the computer. Reproduction of the copyrighted work exists regardless of the number of copies made, technique by which the work is multiplied or the durability of the copy. The Copyright and Neighbouring Rights Act stipulates that the notion of reproduction also cover the operation of the program on the computer. Further to this, the author of the computer program has the exclusive right to authorize or prohibit reproduction of the computer program which was made as a result of adaptation, translation, arrangement or alteration of his computer program, without prejudice to the rights of the person who has made such changes.

B. The Distribution Right

49. The distribution right is defined as the exclusive right to put on the market the original or the copies of the copyrighted work by offering it for sale or offering it in another way to the public for the same purpose. The distribution right also comprises offering copies of the work for the purposes of placing it in circulation, storing copies of the work for the purposes of placing it in circulation, importing copies of the work.

C. The Right of Rental

50. The author has the exclusive right to permit or prohibit rental of the originals or copies of his/her work. The notion of rental is understood as making the original or the copies of the work available for use to other persons for a limited period of time and for the purpose of realizing direct or indirect pecuniary benefit. The author who licensed its right to a producer of phonograms and/or videograms retains the right to obtain an equitable remuneration for the rental of the work. The right of rental may not be exercised in respect of a constructed work of architecture, a work of applied art materialized in the form of an industrial or artisan product, and a work that was made or reproduced for the sole purpose of being rented as agreed upon between the author and owner of a copy of the work.

D. The Right of Representation

51. The author has the exclusive right to authorize or prohibit public performance of his/her work. The right of representation is structured in a two-fold way. The first aspect concerns the right to perform, where the performance is understood as any means of public communication of non-stage works (speech, music) live to the audience. The second aspect concerns the right to present, where the presentation is understood as any means of public communication of stage works (dramatic, dramatic-musical, choreographic, pantomimic works) live to the audience.

E. The Right to Transmit Public Performance of a Work by Means of Technical Devices

52. The Copyright and Neighbouring Rights Act prescribes that the author has the exclusive right to authorize or prohibit the transmission of the performance or presentation of his/her work. The act of transmission is defined as simultaneous public communication of a work that is being performed or presented to the audience present outside the premises on which the work is being performed or presented live, by means of technical devices, such as a loudspeaker or a screen and a loudspeaker.

F. The Right of Broadcasting and Re-broadcasting

53. The author has the exclusive right to authorize or prohibit broadcasting and re-broadcasting of his/her work. The Copyright and Neighbouring Rights Act defines broadcasting as an act of communication to the public of the work of authorship by transmission of radio or television programme-carrying signals from broadcaster entity (broadcasting organization) to receiving devices by network of transmitters (terrestrial broadcasting), cable distribution systems (cable broadcasting) or satellite stations (satellite broadcasting). Under the Copyright and Neighbouring Rights Act, author and/or holder of the copyright has exclusive right to authorize or prohibit retransmission and cable retransmission of its work of authorship. Retransmission is defined as simultaneous communication to the public of work of authorship in unaltered and unabridged way by the person different from the broadcasting organization that originally transmits the work of authorship. Cable retransmission, which occurs by cable or microwave system, is defined as simultaneous, unaltered and unabridged retransmission of initial wire, wireless or satellite transmission of television or radio programmes that is intended for reception by the public. In the case of cable retransmission, author and/or holder of the copyright exercises its right only collectively.

G. The Right of Making Available to the Public of a Work in an Interactive Way

54. In line with the rules laid down by the WIPO Internet Treaties and the EU Directive on Copyright and Related Rights in the Information Society, the Copyright and Neighbouring Rights Act prescribes the exclusive right of an author to communicate to the public his/her work by wire or wireless means, including the making available to the public of a work in such a way that members of the public may access the work from a place and at a time individually chosen by them.

H. *The Right of Adaptation*

55. Under the Copyright and Neighbouring Rights Act, the author has the exclusive right to prohibit or authorize any act of adaptation, arrangement or other alteration of his/her work.

I. *The Right of Public Communication of a Broadcasted Work*

56. The author has the exclusive right to permit or prohibit any act of communication of his/her work that is being broadcasted or re-broadcasted simultaneously to audience at public places. Such public communication of a broadcasted work may, for example, take place in public transportation, restaurants, waiting rooms and the like, by means of such devices as radio receivers or television sets.

J. *The Right of Public Communication of a Work Fixed in an Audio and/or Visual Medium*

57. The author has the exclusive right of permitting or prohibiting the communication to the public of his/her work fixed in an audio and/or visual medium (a record, compact disc, audio cassette, video cassette, film tape, optic disc, slide) by means of technical devices for the reproduction of sound and/or picture.

III. Author's Rights in Relation to the Owner of a Copyrighted Work

58. Certain rights of an author cannot be categorized neither as pecuniary rights of an author nor as moral rights of an author. Due to their complex nature, consisting both of economic and (some) personal characteristics, they form the special category of 'other rights of an author'. These are:

- the right of access to a work;
- the resale right / *droit de suite*;
- the right to prevent public presentation of a work;
- the author's priority right of modification of a work of architecture;
- the right to levy; and
- the right to remuneration for public lending.

A. *Right to Levy*

59. In line with the limitations of the exclusive pecuniary right of reproduction, the work of an author may be reproduced for private or other personal use in the absence of the author's consent. The authors of works, which in view of their nature, can be expected to be reproduced for personal non-commercial purposes on sound, picture and text carriers have the right to remuneration paid in case of import and/or sale of technical devices and sound, picture and text carriers, for which it can be assumed that they shall be used for such reproduction. In addition, in case copyright-protected works have been reproduced by means of photocopying or using a similar technique, the author has the right to remuneration from legal or natural persons who provide commercial services of photocopying. This right may be managed only collectively. Debtors are under an obligation to respond to each request for information on the type and quantity of devices/carriers imported or sold, as well as to each request for information on the number of photocopies made presented by the collective management organizations. The Copyright and Neighbouring Rights Act prescribes that a levy needs to be fair, since levy debtors are not users of copyright-protected works and/or subject matter of related rights.

B. Right to Remuneration for Public Lending

60. The author has the right to a '*fair*' remuneration if the original or the copies of his/her work are lent through public libraries or other institutions intended to the public which are engaged in lending on a professional basis. Under the Copyright and Neighbouring Rights Act, lending is understood as an act of giving the originals or copies of the work to be used for a limited period of time, without realizing direct or indirect economic benefit. The author does not have the right to remuneration when works are lent through national libraries, libraries of the public education institutions and public specialized libraries (or when works are mutually lent by these institutions), as well as in case of lending of works of the applied arts and industrial design or works of architecture. This right may only be managed collectively.

C. Right of Access to a Work

61. The author has the right to request the owner of a copy of a work to allow him/her to access the copy, provided such access is necessary for the reproduction of that work and does not represent a threat to justified interests of the owner or the possessor. While allowing the access, the owner or the possessor does not need to hand over the copy of the work to the author.

*D. Resale Right/*Droit De Suite

62. If the original of a work of fine art is being resold, the author has the right to be informed of the sale and the identity of the new owner, as well as to receive a fee on each resale of his/her work of art. Under the notion of fine art, the legislator comprises works of graphic or plastic art such as pictures, drawings, collages, paintings, engravings, prints, lithographs, sculptures, tapestries, works of art made in ceramics or glass, photographs provided that they are made by the author himself or that those copies are considered to be original works of art. Originals of the work of the fine art are also taken to be the multiplied copies of that work (reproductions) if they have been made in the limited number by the author or the person he authorized. Such copies must be numerated in the usual way and signed or in some other manner marked by the author. The resale right applies to 'public sphere', i.e., when a resale includes persons who are professionally engaged in the sale of works of art, such as art galleries or auction houses. The seller, buyer and agent are solidary debtors with respect of a fee payable to the author. The remuneration is calculated as a percentage of a sales price, without taxes. The fee may amount up to 4% of a sales price. However, the legislator prescribed a maximum amount of such fee, at RSD 1,300,000 (approximately EUR 10,500). Within thirty days of the sale, the seller, buyer and agent have a duty to inform the author of the sale, the information on the seller, buyer and agent, and the exact amount of price paid for the original work of art. The fee payable to the author is due within the term of thirty days from the date when the sale has been performed. The author may request from the seller, buyer and/or agent the information necessary for the securing of the payment of the fee within three years from the act of resale. The author cannot waive or dispose of his/her resale right. Such right cannot be subject to enforced performance. The right is inheritable.

E. Right to Prevent Public Presentation of a Work

63. The owner of the original copy of a painting, sculpture or photograph has the right to exhibit such item, regardless of whether the work has already been made available to the public, unless expressly prohibited by the author in writing, at the time original version was disposed of. If the owner of the original copy of a work is a museum, art gallery or a similar public institution, the author cannot prevent public presentation of a work.

F. Author's Priority Right of Modification of a Work of Architecture

64. The owner of a building, which represents a materialized work of architecture, that intends to make certain alterations on the building, has a duty to offer the author to make such alteration first, provided the author is accessible. Once contacted by the owner of the building, the author has a duty to respond within thirty days from the receipt of the offer. However, the author of the work of architecture cannot oppose to alterations which are urgent and justified by safety and technical reasons. In any event, the author's moral rights must be observed.

§7. Limitations and Exceptions to the Scope of Copyright Protection

65. The Copyright and Neighbouring Rights Act prescribes a number of limitations to copyright and neighbouring rights. The Act provides for two different regimes of limitations, one being the suspension of exclusive rights and right to remuneration, and other – the statutory licence.[24] For example, exclusive rights and a right to remuneration are suspended if the work is used for educational purposes or in the course of media coverage, while the statutory licence is prescribed in cases of a three-dimensional reproduction of works permanently displayed in the streets, squares and other open public places. Each time a work of authorship is exploited pursuant to the prescribed limitations on copyright, the name of the author and the source from which the work was taken (publisher of the work, year and place of publication, periodical, newspaper, television or radio station where the work or a part of it was originally published or directly taken from, and the like), must be clearly indicated. The exploitation of a work must conform to the 'three-step test'. Namely, the work may be used in certain special cases; the scope of limitation of exclusive rights must not conflict with a normal exploitation of the work and must not unreasonably prejudice the legitimate interests of the author and/or the right holder.

§8. Duration of Protection

66. Pecuniary rights last for the life of the author and seventy years after his/her death. Pecuniary rights of a co-author expire after seventy years elapse from the death of the co-author that was last to die. In the case of pecuniary rights on musical works with words, the duration of protection is calculated from the death of the last surviving author of the composition or author of the text, regardless of whether those persons are denoted as co-authors, under the condition that the text and the composition have been created for such musical work with words. Pecuniary rights with respect to the work whose author is unknown (anonymous work or work under a pseudonym) expire after seventy years elapse from the date of the work's disclosure. Should the author reveal his/her identity before the expiration of such term, the duration of pecuniary rights shall be calculated as if the author's identity has been known from the date of disclosure of the work. Pecuniary rights in respect of collective works last for seventy years from the date of the lawful publication of the work. Where the term of protection runs from the time of disclosure of the work and where the work was disclosed in instalments, the term of protection runs for each such instalment separately. Moral rights last even after the expiration of the author's pecuniary rights.

§9. Neighbouring Rights

67. Under the Copyright and Neighbouring Rights Act, the rights related to copyright are: (1) right of performers; (2) right of producers of phonograms; (3) right of producers of videograms; (4) right of producers of broadcasts; (5) right of producers of databases; (6) right of publishers. The provisions of the Copyright and Neighbouring Rights Act related to the publishing and communication to the public of a copyrighted work apply to neighbouring rights *mutatis mutandis*. As a rule,

24. *See,* Copyright and Neighbouring Rights Act, Arts 41–57.

neighbouring rights have only an economic component, whereas their owner does not have moral rights. The only exception is the right of performers, consisting of both economic and moral components. Neighbouring rights are transferable, with the exception of the performers' moral rights.

I. Right of Performers

68. Under the Copyright and Neighbouring Rights Act, performers enjoy moral and pecuniary rights in relation to their performance. A performer is an individual who engages in the performance of works (a musician, actor, dancer, performer of pantomimes, singer, conductor). Persons making only a technical contribution to the performance of works are not considered performers. A performance is defined as an intellectual commodity that originates from personal engagement of a performer during audio, visual or audio-visual communication of the author's work.

69. Pecuniary rights of the performer last for fifty years from the date of the performance. If a performance was recorded and lawfully published or communicated to the public within this period in a different way distinctive from a phonogram, the term of protection shall expire fifty years from the date of the first publication or communication to the public, whichever date is earlier. If within the term of fifty years from the date of the creation of the performance, that performance has been recorded on the phonogram that is lawfully published or lawfully communicated to the public, the right of the performer shall last for seventy years from the date of first lawful publication or communication to the public, depending on which date comes first. A performer's moral rights last even after the expiration of his/her pecuniary rights.

II. Right of Producers of Phonograms

70. Phonogram producers have pecuniary rights in relation to their phonograms. A phonogram is any recording of a sound and/or a sequence of sounds on a sound carrier. A producer of phonogram is any natural or legal person who has organized and financed the production of the phonogram, and that bears the responsibility for the first recording of a sound or a sequence of sounds.

71. The right of the producer of phonograms shall last fifty years from the date of the fixation of the phonogram, if in that period the phonogram has not been lawfully published or communicated to the public. If the phonogram has been lawfully published or communicated to the public during that term, the right expires seventy years from the date of the first lawful publication or disclosure, depending on which date comes first.

III. Right of Producers of Videograms

72. Videogram producers have pecuniary rights in relation to their videograms. A videogram is a recording of a film work, as well as a definite sequence of motion pictures with or without the accompanying sound on the carrier of picture, or the carrier of picture and sound. A producer of videogram (film producer) is any natural or legal person who has, acting on one's own behalf, taken the initiative, gathered financial means, organized, managed and taken the responsibility for the first recording of a film or motion pictures accompanied by a sound or without a sound.

73. The right of the producer of videograms shall last fifty years from the date of fixation of the videogram, if in that term the videogram has not been lawfully published or communicated to the public. If the videogram has been lawfully published or communicated to the public during that term, the right expires fifty years from the date of the publication or communication to the public depending on which date comes first.

IV. Right of Producers of Broadcasts

74. Producers of broadcasts have pecuniary rights in relation to their broadcasts. A producer of a broadcast is any natural or legal person who has organized and financed the production of a broadcast. Under the Copyright and Neighbouring Rights Act, a broadcast is defined as an electrical, electromagnetic or another signal converted into audio, visual or audio-visual content that is broadcasted for the purpose of being communicated to the public.

75. The rights of the producer of broadcasts last for fifty years from the date of the first broadcasting of the protected broadcast.

V. Right of Producers of Databases

76. Under the Copyright and Neighbouring Rights Act, producers of databases enjoy pecuniary rights in relation to their databases. A database is a collection of independent data, works of authorship or other materials arranged in a systematic or methodical way, individually accessible by electronic or other means. The protection of databases does not encompass computer programs which are used for the elaboration of the database or work with databases available by electronic means. A producer of a database is any natural or legal person who has made a substantial investment, in qualitative and/or quantitative sense, in obtaining, verification or presentation of the contents of a database.

77. The right of producers of databases lasts for fifteen years from the date of the creation of a database. If a database was made available to the public in whatever manner before the expiry of that term, the term of protection shall expire fifteen years from the date when database was first made available to the public. Any substantial, qualitative or quantitative change of the content of the database, including any substantial change which comes out as a consequence of permanent additions, deletions or alterations, and which would result in the database being considered for substantially, in a qualitative or quantitative sense, new investment, shall qualify that database to have its own term of protection.

VI. Right of Publishers

78. Under the Copyright and Neighbouring Rights Act, any person who, after the expiry of protection of the author's pecuniary rights, for the first time lawfully publishes or communicates to the public a previously unpublished work, has the rights equivalent to pecuniary rights of the author. The duration of the right of the publisher of previously unpublished work is twenty-five years from the date of the first publication or first communication to the public.

79. The publishers of printed editions have the right to levy under the same conditions which are valid for the authors. The right of publishers of printed editions to levy lasts for fifty years from the lawful publication of the work.

§10. Infringement and Remedies

80. The infringement of copyright and neighbouring rights may result in civil and criminal remedies. Civil law remedies are primarily regulated by the Copyright and Neighbouring Rights Act.[25]

81. A copyright and neighbouring rights infringement consists in any act of unauthorized exploitation of the subject matter of protection, and/or in non-observance of the duty to remunerate the right owner for any authorized act of exploitation of the subject matter of protection, and/or in non-observance of other obligations due to the owner of copyright and neighbouring rights as prescribed by the Act. An infringement of copyright/neighbouring right may also consist of:

- exploitation of the subject matter of protection involving the use of copies of such subject matter of protection that was made without authorization, and/or are based on the unauthorized broadcasting;
- holding copies of the work of authorship or subject matter of neighbouring right for commercial purposes, if the holder knows or has reason to know that such copies are produced without authorization;
- production, import, marketing, sale, rental, advertising for the purposes of sale or rental, or holding for commercial purposes of the devices, products, composite parts, computer programs primarily constructed, produced or adjusted for enabling or facilitating the circumvention of any efficient technological measure;

25. *See* Copyright and Neighboring Rights Act, Arts 204–214.

- circumvention of any technological measure, or supply or advertising of services enabling or facilitating such circumvention;
- removal or alteration of the electronic information regarding rights, or marketing, import, broadcasting or public communication in any other manner of the work of authorship or the subject matter of the neighbouring rights, from which the electronic information on rights is removed or altered without authorization, where the perpetrator knows or has reason to know that by doing so he induces, enables, facilitates or conceals infringement of copyright or neighbouring right.

82. The complaint on the grounds of copyright/neighbouring rights infringement may be filed by the copyright owner, performer, phonogram producer, videogram producer, broadcast producer, database producer, the acquirer of exclusive rights on the subject matter of protection, as well as organization for collective management of copyright and neighbouring rights. In case of copyright/neighbouring rights infringement or in case of existence of serious threat that the right shall be infringed, the plaintiff may request *inter alia*:

- that infringement of the right be determined;
- cessation of the infringement of right;
- that the articles used in infringement of the right be destroyed or modified;
- that the tools and equipment used for production of the articles used in infringement of the right be destroyed or modified, if that is necessary for the efficient protection of the right;
- compensation for material damages and reasonable costs of procedure (except in case of constructed works of architecture);
- information on any third persons participating in infringement of the right to be revealed;
- publication of the court decision in the press.

The person infringing copyright/neighbouring rights is held liable for the injury pursuant to the general rules on compensation of damages. In determining the amount of compensation for damage when the infringer knew or could have known that he infringes the right, the court shall take into account all circumstances of the particular case, such as negative economic consequences which the injured party has suffered, including lost profits, profits of the infringer acquired by infringement of right, as well as, in adequate cases, circumstances which do not have economic nature, such as non-economic damage. The court may, when the circumstances of particular case allow, adjudge to the injured party the lump sum compensation which cannot be lower than the usual compensation which he would have received for particular use of subject matter of protection, if the use was lawful. Only authors and performers may request compensation for moral damages (compensation for infringement of moral rights).

83. The court may order an interim measure at the request of the person who makes it credible that the copyright/neighbouring right has been infringed, or that such infringement is imminent. The interim measure may consist, *inter alia,* in the seizure or withdrawal from circulation of the articles used in infringement, or the measure of prohibiting continuation of any activities by way of which the infringement may be/is committed. Further to this type of interim measure, the court may also comply with the request of the person who makes it credible that the copyright/neighbouring right has been infringed, or that such infringement is imminent, or that irreparable harm is likely to occur, or that there is a reasonable suspicion that evidence will be destroyed or that it will not be possible to collect it later, to order an interim measure to secure evidence without giving prior notice to, or hearing the person from whom the evidence is to be collected. The securing of evidence is being realized through the inspection of premises, vehicles, books, documents, as well as the seizure of documents and infringing goods, questioning of witnesses and expert witnesses. Both types of measures may be requested even before filing a complaint, provided that subsequently a complaint is filed within thirty days from the date of rendering the decision on interim measure/on securing the evidence.

84. The Copyright and Neighbouring Rights Act prescribes that the provisions of the Civil Procedure Act[26] and the Enforcement Act[27] are to be applied by analogy. Also, damages-related claims should be resolved by application of provisions of the Contract and Torts Act.[28]

85. Further to civil law remedies, the Copyright and Neighbouring Rights Act lists certain types of conduct that are subject to criminal penalties. Namely, a legal person who has infringed a copyright or a neighbouring right is sanctioned on grounds of corporate offence (in Serbian, *privredni prestup*) by a fine. The infringing activity may in particular consist of:

- disclosing, recording, reproducing or communicating to the public in any manner wholly or partly, a work of authorship, performance, phonogram, videogram, broadcast or database without permission, or marketing or renting or holding in possession in commercial purposes copies of works of authorship, performances of phonograms, videograms, broadcasts or databases that have been reproduced or placed on the market without authorization;
- marketing or renting of the copies of subject matter of protection, for the purpose of deriving pecuniary benefit for itself or somebody else, knowing that they were disclosed, recorded or reproduced without authorization;
- producing, importing, marketing, selling, renting, advertising for the purposes of sale or renting, or holding for commercial purposes devices, products, composite parts, computer programs primarily constructed, produced or adjusted for enabling or facilitating the circumvention of any efficient technological measure, which do not have any other significant purpose than the said one;
- circumventing any efficient technological measure, or supplying or advertising the services which enable or facilitate such circumvention;

26. Official Journal of the Republic of Serbia, n° 72/2011, 49/2013, 74/2013, 55/2014, 87/2018 and 18/2020.
27. *Ibid.*, n° 06/2015, 106/2016, 113/2017 and 54/2019.
28. Official Journal of the SFR Yugoslavia, n° 29/78, 39/85, 45/89; Official Journal of the FR Yugoslavia, n° 31/93; Official Journal of the Union of Serbia and Montenegro, n° 1/2003; Official Journal of the Republic of Serbia, n° 18/2020.

- removing or altering electronic information on rights, or marketing, importing, broadcasting or in any other manner communicating the work of authorship or the subject matter of neighbouring right to the public, from which the electronic information on rights has illegally been removed or altered, while knowing or having reason to know that by doing so it instigates, enables, facilitates or conceals the infringement of a copyright or neighbouring right;
- making an alteration on the building which represents a materialized copy of the work of architecture without prior offering the author to do the alterations of the work;
- not submitting to the collective management organization of the data on the title of the subject matter of protection, frequency and scope of utilization, as well as other circumstances which are relevant for the calculation and distribution of the remuneration that must be paid according to the tariff;
- not keeping the electronic record of broadcasting and retransmitting of works of authorship and subject matter of neighbouring rights;
- conducting collective exercise of copyright and/or neighbouring rights without permission of the competent authority.

A responsible person in a legal entity who is found to infringe copyright/neighbouring right may also be fined. The infringing objects and the objects used for the perpetration of the corporate offence may be forfeited and the infringing objects may be destroyed. An entrepreneur or any natural person who has infringed a copyright/neighbouring right is sanctioned on grounds of misdemeanour (in Serbian, *prekršaj*) by a fine. The infringing objects in a misdemeanour and the objects used for perpetration of the misdemeanour may be forfeited and the infringing objects may be destroyed.

86. A legal person may be sanctioned on ground of misdemeanour by a fine if he:

- without stating the author's or performer's name or under different name, wholly or partially discloses, performs, presents, communicates the performance or presentation or broadcasts work of authorship or performance of another person;
- without permission of the author modifies or adapts work of authorship or recorded performance of another person;
- in the capacity of the professional art dealer (sales saloons, art galleries, auction houses, etc.), in the term of thirty days from the date of sale of the original work of the fine art, does not inform the author of the work on the title and name and address of the salesman, agent and buyer of his work, and the price for which the work has been sold, and does not pay to the author the remuneration prescribed by the law (infringement of *droit de suite*);
- gives incorrect data or deceives true data about its work of authorship or subject matter of neighbouring rights when entering into the records and depositing work of authorship or subject matter of neighbouring right with the Intellectual Property Office (IP Office);
- as a publisher sells the unsold copies of the work as scrap paper without previously offering it to the author or his/her heirs for purchase;

- does not enable to the persons who, on the basis of the provisions of the Copyright Act on the limitations of copyright, have legal access to the copies of work or subject matter of neighbouring rights to benefit from the substantive limitations of rights, by alteration or removal of technological measures or in some other way; and
- on the copy of work or subject matter of neighbouring rights elaborated or imported for commercial purposes, does not indicate clearly and visibly the use of technological measures.

A responsible person in a legal entity who is found to infringe copyright/neighbouring right may also be fined. An entrepreneur or a natural person may also be fined if they engage in one of these activities.

87. The Penal Code prescribes criminal responsibility for acts of unauthorized exploitation of a copyrighted work or subject matter of neighbouring rights.[29] Namely, a person who, without permission publishes, records, copies or otherwise makes available to the public, in part or entirety, a copyrighted work, performance, phonogram, videogram, broadcast, computer program or database, shall be punished with a fine or imprisonment up to three years. The same punishment shall also be imposed on a person who puts into circulation or keeps copies of copyrighted work, performance, phonogram, videogram, broadcast, computer program or database which are illegally multiplied or illegally put into circulation. If the offence was committed with intent to acquire material gain for oneself or another, the offender shall be punished with imprisonment from three months to five years. Furthermore, a person who produces, imports, puts into circulation, sells, rents, advertises for sale or rent, or keeps for commercial purposes, equipment and devices whose basic or prevailing purpose is to remove, bypass or forestall technological measures intended for prevention of violation of copyright and neighbouring rights, or who uses such equipment or devices with an aim to violate copyright or neighbouring right, shall be punished with a fine or imprisonment up to three years. A person who, without the authorization from the right owner, removes or alters electronic information on copyright or neighbouring right, or puts into circulation, imports, exports, broadcasts or otherwise makes available to the public a copyrighted work or a subject matter of neighbouring right, from which electronic information on rights was removed or altered without authorization, shall be punished with a fine and imprisonment up to three years. Finally, the Penal Code prescribes criminal responsibility for acts of infringement of moral rights of authors and performers. A person who under his/her name or the name of another publishes or puts into circulation copies of another's copyrighted work or performance or otherwise publicly presents another's copyrighted work or performance, in entirety or in part, shall be punished with a fine or imprisonment up to three years. A person who, without the author's permission, alters or adapts another's copyrighted work or alters

29. *See* Penal Code, Official Journal of the Republic of Serbia, n° 85/2005, 88/2005, 107/2005, 72/2009, 111/2009, 121/2009, 104/2013, 108/2014, 94/2016 and 35/2019, Arts 198–200. For a detailed analysis of criminal offenses against intellectual property *see*: Z. Stojanović, N. Delić, *Krivično pravo-Posebni deo,* Pravni fakultet Univerziteta u Beogradu, Pravna knjiga, Belgrade 2013, 123–133.

another's recorded performance, shall be punished with a fine or imprisonment up to one year. A person who puts into circulation copies of another's copyrighted work or performance in a manner which is harmful to the honour and reputation of the author or performer, shall be punished with a fine or imprisonment up to six months. In case of infringement of the right to oppose the unbecoming exploitation of the work, the proceedings are not initiated ex officio.

§11. OVERLAPPING AND RELATION TO OTHER INTELLECTUAL PROPERTY RIGHTS

88. In Serbian intellectual property law, a design may be protected by both a copyright and an industrial design right, provided that it meets different criteria prescribed by the Copyright and Neighbouring Rights Act, on the one hand, and the Industrial Design Act, on the other hand.

The owner of rights with regard to such designs under the Copyright and Neighbouring Rights Act and the Industrial Design Act may choose to exercise the rights and legal actions derived from one or the other intellectual property, in a given case, but may not simultaneously claim protection under both regimes.[30]

30. *See* Ch. 6, §10.

Chapter 2. Patents

§1. Sources – Legislation

89. The development of the national patent law started in 1920, when the Kingdom of Serbs, Croats and Slovenes adopted the Regulation on the protection of industrial property. The Regulation was the first source of national law regulating the legal protection of inventions. The Regulation was soon replaced by the first Industrial Property Act, adopted in 1922. The Act, amended in 1928, was in force until World War II. The Act was drafted in line with the provisions of the Paris Convention on the Protection of Industrial Property (1884). The Kingdom of Serbia was among eleven countries that signed and ratified the Convention in 1883–1884.[31]

90. In the socialist Yugoslavia, the first act regulating the protection of inventions that was adopted following World War II was the Act on inventions and technical improvements. The Act was adopted in 1948, under the strong influence of the Soviet law. Inventions made by domestic citizens were to be protected under the 'inventor's certificate', while the patent protection *stricto sensu* was intended for inventions made by foreigners. The modernization of Serbian (Yugoslav) patent law started in 1960, when the new Act on patents and technical improvements was adopted. This Act abolished the Soviet-modelled system of protection of inventions, based on 'inventors' certificates', and introduced patent protection as the only form of legal protection of inventions. In 1981, the new Act on the protection of inventions, technical improvements and indications of geographical origin was adopted. The Act was later amended in 1990 and remained in force until 1995, when the new Patent Act was adopted. In that period, Serbia was experiencing significant structural and constitutional changes. The Socialist Federal Republic of Yugoslavia was succeeded by the Federal Republic of Yugoslavia in 1992. The latter was succeeded by the State Union of Serbia and Montenegro in 2003. The State Union of Serbia and Montenegro adopted its Patent Act in 2004. Following the dissolution of the State Union, the act remained in force in the RS. It was replaced in 2011 by the new Patent Act, which was amended in 2017, 2018 and 2019.[32]

31. Signature of the Paris Convention (1883) by the Kingdom of Serbia: 20 Mar. 1883; Ratification: 6 Jun. 1884; Entry into force: 7 Jul. 1884. Signature of the Brussels Act (1900): 14 Dec. 1900; Accession: 23 Aug. 1909; Entry into force: 10 Oct. 1909. Accession to the Washington Act (1911) by the Kingdom of Serbs, Croats and Slovenes: 4 Jan. 1921; Entry into force: 26 Feb. 1921. Signature of the Hague Act (1925): 6 Nov. 1925; Accession: 22 Aug. 1928; Entry into force: 29 Oct. 1928. Signature of the London Act (1934) by the Kingdom of Yugoslavia: 2 Jun. 1934; Accession by the Socialist Federal Republic of Yugoslavia: 18 Mar. 1965; Entry into force: 7 Jun. 1965. Signature of the Lisbon Act (1958) by the Federal People's Republic of Yugoslavia: 31 Oct. 1958; Accession by the Socialist Federal Republic of Yugoslavia: 22 Dec. 1964; Entry into force: 11 Apr. 1965. Signature of the Stockholm Act (1967): 14 Jul. 1967; Ratification: 11 Jul. 1973; Entry into force: 16 Oct. 1973. Declaration of succession by Federal Republic of Yugoslavia: 14 Jun. 2001; Entry into force: 27 Apr. 1992. Declaration of continuation by the Republic of Serbia: 19 Sep. 2006.
32. Official Journal of the Republic of Serbia, n° 99/2011, 113/2017, 95/2018 and 66/2019.

91. With respect to the registration procedure, the Government of Serbia adopted the Regulations on the content of certificates, applications and requests in the procedure of the protection of inventions, as well as the manner of filing the application and publication of inventions (hereinafter, the Regulation).[33] The National Registry of Patents is available on the website of the IP Office.[34]

92. Further to the Paris Convention, the RS is party to several specialized international conventions in the area of patent protection:

- Patent Cooperation Treaty (PCT).[35]
- Budapest Treaty on the International Recognition of the Deposit of Microorganisms for the Purposes of Patent Procedure.[36]
- Strasbourg Agreement Concerning the International Patent Classification.[37]
- Patent Law Treaty.[38]
- Convention on the Grant of European Patents (European Patent Convention).[39]

Therefore, the RS may be a designated country in a PCT application or in a European patent application.

§2. Subject Matter of Protection

93. Under the Patent Act, and in line with the provisions of the European Patent Convention, any invention in any field of technology, which is new, involves an inventive step and is susceptible of industrial application, may be protected by a patent in Serbia.[40] The following, in particular, shall not be regarded as inventions, within the meaning of the Patent Act:

- discoveries, scientific theories and mathematical methods;
- aesthetic creations;
- schemes, rules and methods for performing mental acts, playing games or doing;
- business;
- computer programs; and

33. *Ibid.*, n° 78/2019.
34. The Registry is available at: *http://www.zis.gov.rs* .
35. Accession by the Federal Republic of Yugoslavia: 1 Feb. 1997. Official Journal of the Federal Republic of Yugoslavia – International Treaties, n° 3/96.
36. Accession by the Federal Republic of Yugoslavia: 25 Nov. 1993; Entry into force: 25 Feb. 1994. Declaration of continuation by Republic of Serbia: 19 Sep. 2006. Official Journal of the Federal Republic of Yugoslavia – International Treaties, n° 3/93.
37. Signature by the Socialist Federal Republic of Yugoslavia: 24 Mar. 1971; Ratification by the Republic of Serbia: 15 Jul. 2009; Entry into force: 15 Jul. 2010. Official Journal of the Republic of Serbia – International Treaties, n° 42/09.
38. Accession by the Republic of Serbia: 20 May 2010; Entry into force: 20 Aug. 2010. Official Journal of the Republic of Serbia – International Treaties, n° 19/10.
39. The Republic of Serbia joined the European Patent Organization (EPO) on 1 Oct. 2010. Official Journal of the Republic of Serbia – International Treaties, n° 5/10.
40. *See* Patent Act, Arts 7–9; European Patent Convention, Arts 52–53.

– presentations of information.

Subject matter or activities are excluded from patentability only to the extent to which the patent application relates to the subject matter or activity as such. In Serbia, the human body, at any stage of its formation and development, and the simple discovery of one of its elements, including sequences or partial sequences of genes, is not regarded as invention that can be protected by a patent. However, an element isolated from the human body or produced by means of a technical process, including the sequences or partial sequences of genes, may be patentable, even where the structure of that element is identical to that of a natural element.

94. Certain inventions containing biological material are patentable. Patent may be granted for an invention for a product consisting of or containing biological material, or the process of which biological material is produced, processed or used, including:

– a biological material isolated from its natural environment or produced by means of a technical process, even if it previously occurred in nature;
– plants or animals, if the technical feasibility of the invention is not confined to a particular plant or animal variety; and
– a microbiological or other technical process or a product obtained by means of such a process.

'Biological material' within the meaning of the Patent Act should be understood as any material containing genetic information and capable of reproducing itself or being reproduced in a biological system.

95. The Patent Act prescribes certain exceptions to patentability. The following inventions cannot be protected by a patent or petty patent:

(1) inventions whose commercial use would be contrary to public order or morality, particularly in respect of:
   – processes for cloning human beings;
   – processes for modifying the genetic identity of germ cells of human beings;
   – uses of human embryos for industrial or commercial purposes; and
   – processes for modifying the genetic identity of animals which are likely to cause them suffering without any substantial medical benefit to man or animal, and also animals resulting from such processes;
(2) inventions concerning methods for treatment by surgery or diagnostic methods or therapy practised directly on the human or animal body, provided that this rule is not applied to products or substances and compositions for use in any of these methods;
(3) plant or animal variety or an essentially biological process for the production of a plant or animal, provided that this rule is not applied to microbiological processes or the products obtained by means of such process.

The Patent Act defines an essentially biological process as a process which consists entirely of natural phenomena such as crossing or selection. A microbiological process is defined as any process involving or performed upon or resulting in microbiological material.

§3. Conditions of Protection

96. Under the Patent Act, patents may be granted for any inventions, in all fields of technology, provided that they are new, involve an inventive step and are susceptible to industrial application.[41] The prescribed patentability requirements are harmonized with the criteria laid down by the European Patent Convention and existing in comparative patent law.

97. The novelty requirement is defined with respect to the notion of the 'state of the art'. Namely, an invention is considered new if it does not form part of the state of the art. The state of the art is held to comprise:

- everything made available to the public by means of written or oral description, by use or in any other way, prior to the date of the filing of an application for a protection of an invention;
- the content of all applications in the RS as filed, with the filing date preceding the date of the filing of an application for a protection of an invention and published on or after that date.

The public disclosure of the invention by any person, including the patent applicant, before filing a patent application therefore destroys novelty and the ability to obtain a valid patent in Serbia. Consequently, the RS operates an 'absolute novelty' requirement. Public disclosures can include written or electronic publications, public demonstrations, public oral disclosures, public use… This however does not exclude the possibility for patent protection of substances or compositions included in the state of the art, for use in a method of treatment by surgery or diagnostic method or therapy, provided their use for these methods is not comprised in the state of the art. Furthermore, the cited rule should not be understood as to exclude the possibility for patent protection of substances or compositions for any specific use in a method of treatment by surgery or diagnostic method or therapy, provided such use for these methods is not comprised in the state of the art.

98. In certain situations, prescribed by the Patent Act, disclosures of the invention should not be taken into consideration. Such 'non-prejudicial disclosures' may arise if an invention, which was already part of the state of the art for a period of up to six months before the filing of the application, is disclosed due to or as a consequence of:

- evident abuse in relation to the applicant or his legal predecessor;

41. *See* Patent Act, Arts 10–13.

– the invention being displayed by the applicant or his legal predecessor at an official, or officially recognized exhibition, falling within the terms of the Convention on International Exhibitions, signed in Paris on 22 November 1928, and last revised on 30 November 1972, provided that the applicant states, when filing the application, that the invention was exhibited and that he provides an appropriate certificate to support this statement within a period of four months from the filing date of the application.

The certificate confirming that an exhibition or a fair organized in the RS was of an officially recognized international character is issued by the Serbian Chamber of Commerce.

99. Inventive step is the second patentability requirement prescribed by the Patent Act. Namely, an invention is considered to involve an inventive step if, having regard to the state of the art, it is not obvious to a person skilled in the appropriate art. The legal standard of a 'person skilled in the art' should be understood as referring to a skilled practitioner in the relevant field of technology, who is in possession of average knowledge and ability and is aware of what was common general knowledge in the art at the relevant date. Common general knowledge can come from various sources (technical journal, textbook, monograph, etc). An assertion that something is common general knowledge need only be backed by documentary evidence if this is contested. An obvious invention within the meaning of the Patent Act would be any invention which does not go beyond the normal progress of technology but merely follows from the prior art. For example, an obvious invention would be the one which does not involve the exercise of any skill or ability beyond that to be expected of the person skilled in the art.

100. The final patentability requirement relates to industrial application of an invention. This requirement is interpreted broadly. Namely, an invention is considered to be susceptible to industrial application if its subject matter can be made or used in any kind of industry, including agriculture. In most cases, the way in which the invention can be exploited in industry is self-evident and need not further be explained. However, there may be inventions in relation to methods of testing, where the manner of industrial exploitation is not apparent and must therefore be explicitly indicated. This is also the case with respect to certain biotechnological inventions (e.g., sequences and partial sequences of genes).

§4. Formalities: Procedure for Obtaining Protection

101. Protection of inventions is obtained by means of registration before the IP Office. Since the RS opted for the deferred patent examination system, the procedure for obtaining protection is conducted in two separate phases. The IP Office first formally examines a patent application. Following the publication of a patent application, the applicant may initiate the examination of substantial requirements for obtaining patent protection.

I. Patent Application

102. The procedure before the IP Office is initiated by filling an application for a patent registration. A patent is vested in an inventor, or in his legal successor, or in the employer in specific cases prescribed by the law. If an invention is the result of the joint effort of a number of inventors, they have a joint right to protection. A person rendering technical assistance to an inventor is not considered to be an inventor. If two or more persons have filed an application for a protection of the joint invention, it is considered, unless otherwise stipulated by them, that their aliquot parts are equal.

103. Foreign natural and legal persons enjoy the national treatment if it results from international agreements or under reciprocity principle. A party invoking reciprocity between Serbia and a foreign country is supposed to submit the proof of its existence. Foreign natural and legal persons who have no residence or seat in Serbia must be represented by a local attorney or agent registered within the IP Office. However, a foreign natural or legal person may act individually in the following situations:

- filing of an application and performing other actions for the purposes of the accordance of the filing date of application;
- paying the fees and procedural costs.

In such cases, a foreign natural or legal person must appoint a representative for correspondence who has an address in the territory of RS.

104. The legal regime of inventions made in the course of employment requires further clarification. The Patent Act differentiates between two categories of inventions made in the course of employment.[42] The first category corresponds to inventions: (1) made by an employee while performing tasks established by an employment contract concluded between the employee and the employer; or (2) which have been created in compliance with the separate act of the employer regulating tasks of the research and development. The second category corresponds to inventions that have been created during the term of the employment contract or in the period of one year from the date of the termination of the contract, provided that: (1) the invention has been created in connection with the activities of the employer; or (2) the invention is made with the use of material and technical facilities, information and other working conditions provided by the employer; or (3) the invention was created as the result of professional training that the employer secured for the employee. The right to the protection of an invention is vested in the employer, unless otherwise provided by contract between the inventor and employer. If an invention made in the course of employment has been protected in the name of the employer, the inventor has moral rights related to the invention and is entitled to remuneration. Criteria for determining the amount of remuneration and the method

42. *Ibid.*, 57–66.

and time of payment are to be established by a general act or an employment agreement or by a special agreement concluded between the employer and employee with regard to the specific invention. In case no such act or agreement is concluded, the compensation is determined in every individual case taking into consideration: (1) the economic and other contributions arising out of the utilization of the invention by the employer or by the third parties, with the consent of the employee; (2) contribution of the employer in the creation of the invention; in particular facilities that have been placed at the disposal of the employee; (3) individual contribution of every inventor, in case when the invention has been created by several employees. In the absence of the agreement between the employer and employee with regard to the compensation, the competent court, at the request of either the employer or the employee, shall decide on the amount and manner of payment of compensation. The Patent Act prescribes specific procedures to be followed by both the employer and the employee in case of an invention is made in the course of employment. An employee who comes up with an invention in the course of employment is required to submit a written report to the employer immediately upon the creation of the invention, informing him thereof. On the other hand, the employer has the obligation to inform the employee in writing if he intends to file the patent application or not.

105. A patent application is to be written in Serbian language. However, the Patent Act allows for the application to be filed in a foreign language, provided that the applicant subsequently submits the translation into Serbian. A patent application must contain the following elements:

- a request for the grant of right;
- a description of the invention;
- one or more patent claims for the protection of an invention;
- a drawing referred to in the description and/or claims; and
- an abstract.

A request for the grant of right must contain an explicit indication whether a patent or petty patent is being sought, data concerning the applicant, data concerning the inventor or a statement to the effect that the inventor does not wish to be mentioned in the application, and the title of the invention which shall clearly and concisely state the technical designation of the invention. The IP Office does not investigate whether the applicant is entitled to file the patent application. If the applicant is not the inventor or is not the sole inventor, it shall be required to cite the names of all the inventors in the application and to file a statement indicating the legal ground for filing the application. Further to this, an invention must be described in a manner that is clear and complete enough for the invention to be carried out by a person skilled in the art. If the invention concerns a biological material and cannot be carried out on the basis of the description of the invention, this condition will be considered fulfilled if a sample of the naturally reproducible biological material is deposited with a competent depository institution not later than the filing date of the application. Patent claims represent the most important element of each patent application. Patent claims define the subject matter for which the protection is sought. They must be clear, concise and supported by the description of the invention. A patent application must also contain a drawing of an invention for which patent is being sought. Exceptionally, the applicant may submit a photograph instead of a drawing (e.g., micro photos of tissues or cells). Finally, a patent application must contain an abstract, which briefly sets out the essential content of the invention and may serve exclusively to provide technical information. The requirements a patent application must meet are prescribed in a more detailed manner by the Regulation on the content of certificates, applications and requests in the procedure of the protection of inventions, as well as the manner of filing the application and publication of inventions.

106. A patent application cannot contain any text or drawings contrary to public order or public morality, statements that diminish the products or procedures of any third party or quality and the importance of the application or patent of that person, or statements that are obviously not important or necessary.

107. Patent applications submitted to the IP Office are registered in the Registry of patent applications, kept by the Office. The Registry of patent applications includes, in particular: the application number and the application filing date; data on applicant; data on inventor; title of the invention; data on any changes referring to the application (assignment, licence, pledge, etc.). The applicant may request the grant of priority right. Namely, any person who has duly filed an application for any form of protection of an invention in any Member State of the Paris Union for the Protection of Industrial Property or in any Member State of the World Trade Organization (WTO), or its successor in title, shall be granted priority in the RS from the date of the filing the first application, provided that it files a claim to that effect with the IP Office on filing an application for the protection of the same invention, and that the application for the same invention is filed with the IP Office within twelve months from the filing date of the first application. Consequently, the right of priority has the effect that the date of priority counts as the date of filing of the patent application. An applicant who has filed an application for a protection of an invention and who intends to take advantage of the priority of a previous application in the RS must file with the IP Office:

- a priority claim containing essential data concerning the first application claiming priority (application number and filing date, a Member State of the Paris Union or WTO in or for which the application was filed) not later than up to the expiration of two months from the date of filing the application in the RS;
- a copy of the first application certified by the competent authority of the Member State of the Paris Union or WTO in or for which it was filed, not later than up to the expiration of the period of three months of the filing of the application in the RS or sixteen months from the earliest priority date claimed, whichever period expires first.

108. Once the application has been accorded a date of filing, the IP Office shall examine, *inter alia*, whether the filing fee has been paid and the proof of payment has been submitted, whether a valid authorization for the representative or a statement on the appointment of a common representative has been filed (where appropriate), whether the application contains designation of the inventor or a statement to the effect that he/she does not wish to be mentioned in the application; whether a claim for a grant of priority has been filed, whether the content of the application satisfies all requirements prescribed the law ... [43]

109. If a patent application fulfils the requirements laid down by the Patent Act, the IP Office shall invite the applicant to file the request for a search report based on the subject of the invention and to pay the fee for drawing up the search report within one month from the date of the receipt of the invitation. The IP Office shall, upon the receipt of the request and the proof of fee payment, draw up a search report in respect of the patent application on the basis of the claims, with due regard to the description and drawings and shall forward it to the applicant. The IP Office normally publishes the search report together with the patent application. Exceptionally, if the search report cannot be published at the same time as the application, it shall be published separately. The patent application is published in the Official Gazette of the IP Office:

- after the expiry of a period of eighteen months from the date of filing or, if priority has been claimed, from the date of priority; or
- at the request of the applicant, before the expiry of the said period, but not before the expiry of three months from the filing date.

110. Finally, if an application, filled by a national of RS, is found to be important for the defence or security of the country, it will be examined in a different procedure ('secret invention'). Namely, when the IP Office estimates in the course of examination of a patent application that the latter falls under the category of inventions important for the defence or security of the RS it shall forward the application to the Ministry of Defense, and such application shall retain the filing date accorded to it by the IP Office. If the Ministry of Defense finds that the invention for which the protection is sought is not secret, it shall forward the application to the IP Office within three months from its receipt. In the course of examination of an application for a secret invention, the Ministry of Defense may request an expert opinion from the IP Office on whether the secret invention for which the protection is sought is patentable. A secret invention must not be published. A national of the RS may claim protection for a secret invention abroad only on approval of the Ministry of Defense.

43. *See* Patent Act, Art. 99.

II. Grant of a Patent

111. Since the RS opted for the deferred patent examination system, the substantive examination of a patent application may not start until the applicant submits to the IP Office a request for such examination.[44] The request for substantive examination of an application must be filed by the applicant within a period of six months from the date of receipt of the search report. In the event of failure to observe the time limit, the applicant may file the request for substantive examination within an extended period of thirty days from the date of the receipt of a notification of the expiry. The request for substantive examination may not be withdrawn. If no request is made in due time, the IP Office shall render conclusion rejecting the application.

112. In the course of the substantive examination of an application, the IP Office shall examine whether the subject matter of the application:

- constitutes an invention within the meaning of the Patent Act;
- constitutes an invention which is not excluded from the patent protection under the Patent Act;
- meets the requirement of unity of invention;
- is disclosed in a manner sufficiently clear and complete as prescribed by the Patent Act;
- constitutes a technical solution of a specific problem, which is new, involves an inventive step and is susceptible to industrial application; and
- fulfils the conditions for the recognition of a priority right.

The substantive examination of a patent application is conducted within the limits set by the content of the patent claims. If the IP Office establishes that the subject matter of an application does not meet the requirements prescribed by the Patent Act, it shall inform the applicant of the results of examination and invite it, as many times as is necessary, to rectify any deficiencies identified, within a time limit of no less than two months nor more than three months.

113. In the course of substantive examination of a patent application, the IP Office may take into consideration observations submitted by third parties. Namely, following the publication of the patent application, any third party may present observations concerning the patentability of the invention for which the protection is sought. Such observations must be made in writing and state the reasons covering all the grounds against the grant of the patent.

114. If the IP Office establishes that all requirements for the grant of a patent are met, it shall communicate to the applicant a draft of the final wording of the patent claims for adoption and invite the applicant to give his approval within a period of thirty days. If the applicant fails to submit a written statement that he approves the wording and number of claims, within the prescribed time limit, the IP Office shall

44. *Ibid.*, Arts 103–112a.

take a decision to grant a patent on the basis of the final wording of the claims it had communicated for approval. If, on the other hand, the applicant states its disapproval of the wording of the claims, it will be required to state the reasons for the disapproval and to file an amended wording of the claims. If the IP Office accepts the reasons or the amended wording of the claims, it shall take the decision to grant the patent. If it does not accept the said reasons, it shall notify the applicant, stating its grounds thereof, and shall take a decision to grant the patent according to the final wording of the patent claims communicated for approval. Once the proof of payments is submitted, the IP Office shall issue the decision on the grant of a patent, which will subsequently be entered into the Patent Registry. The patent owner shall be issued a patent certificate. The grant of a patent shall be published in the Official Journal of the IP Office.

115. If, following the substantive examination of a patent application, the IP Office establishes that all requirements for the grant of a patent have not been satisfied or that the defects identified have not been remedied, it shall take a decision to refuse the grant of a patent.

§5. Ownership and Transfer: Assignment – Licenses

116. The holder of a patent is an inventor – a natural person who made a patentable invention and submitted a patent application, or his/her legal successors. If an invention is the result of the joint effort of a number of inventors they have a joint right to protection. The particulars of the patent holder are entered into the Patent Registry, administered by the IP Office. Foreign natural and legal persons who have no seat or residence in the RS enjoy the same rights as domestic natural and legal persons, where such treatment derives from international treaties binding on the RS. As already explained, the right to the protection of an invention made by an employee is vested in the employer, unless otherwise provided by a contract between the inventor and employer.[45]

117. The rights granted with regard to a patented invention may be assigned. Assignment of a patent and/or right arising from a patent application may result from the assignment agreement, change of status of the holder of a patent and/or the applicant, inheritance, or a court or administrative decision. Assignment is to be recorded in the appropriate registry of the IP Office. Registration of the assignment produces effects with respect to third parties. In case the assignment results from an assignment agreement, such an agreement must be concluded in written form and contain a designation of contracting parties, patent registration number or the number of patent application, and the amount of remuneration, if stipulated.[46]

45. *See supra* § 4 a).
46. *See* Patent Act, Arts 44–45. General rules on contractual transfer of rights laid down by the Contract and Torts Act are also applicable.

118. The patent owner and/or the applicant may grant licence with respect to the right to use the protected invention and/or invention for which the registration application is submitted, by entering into a licensing agreement. The agreement has to be concluded in writing and contain indication of the contracting parties, patent registration number or patent application number, the term of validity of the licence and the scope of the licence. The licence agreement is to be recorded in the appropriate registry of the IP Office. Registration of the licence agreement produces effects with respect to third parties.[47]

119. The patent or right arising from the patent application may be pledged. The patent owner and/or the applicant may pledge the patent and/or right arising from the patent application by entering into an agreement of pledge. The agreement has to be concluded in written form and is to be recorded in the appropriate registry of the IP Office. Pledge may also result from a court or administrative decision.[48]

§6. Scope of Exclusive Rights

120. The Serbian legislator defines the exclusive rights of the patent holder in a manner similar to the one practised in other European continental jurisdictions. The patent holder has the exclusive right to:

– use the protected invention in production;
– place on the market products made by the protected invention; and
– dispose of the patent.

In exercising its exclusive right to the commercial use of a protected invention, the patent owner has the right to prevent any third party not having his consent from:

– making, offering for sale, placing on the market or using the product made by means of the protected invention or from importing or storing the product for such purposes;
– using the patented process;
– offering the patented process for sale;
– producing, offering for sale, placing on the market, using, importing or storing for such purposes a product directly obtained by the patented process;
– offering for sale or supplying products that constitute essential elements of an invention to parties unauthorized to use such invention, if the offeror or supplier knows or has demonstrable grounds to know that such products are intended for the use of an invention owned by someone else.[49]

---

47. *See* Patent Act, Art. 46. General rules on license agreements laid down by the Contract and Torts Act are also applicable.
48. *See* Patent Act, Art. 47. General rules on pledge of movable assets and rights are also applicable.
49. *See* Patent Act, Art. 14 et seq.

121. If a patent concerns biological material possessing specific characteristics which are the result of a biotechnological invention, the exclusive rights of a patent holder extend to any biological material derived from that biological material through propagation or multiplication, in an identical or divergent form and possessing those same characteristics. If a patent concerns a product containing or consisting of genetic information, the exclusive rights of a patent holder extend to all other material in which the product is incorporated, provided it contains genetic information that performs its function, except the human body at the various stages of its formation and development, and the simple discovery of one of its elements, including the sequence or partial sequence of a gene in which the product is incorporated, provided it contains genetic information that performs its function. If a patent concerns a process that enables a production of biological material possessing specific characteristics as a result of the biotechnological invention, the exclusive rights of a patent holder also extend to biological material directly obtained through the process and to any other biological material derived from the directly obtained biological material through propagation or multiplication, in an identical or divergent form and possessing those same characteristics.

§7. Exceptions and Limitations to the Scope of Patent Protection: Compulsory Licenses

122. The Patent Act prescribes several limitations to exclusive protection of an invention.[50] As it is the case with the subject matter of protection of other intellectual property rights, a patented invention or products made by means of a patented invention may be used by third parties, without consent by the right owner, for personal non-commercial purposes. Further to this, a patent holder cannot prevent others from undertaking research and development activities relating to the subject matter of a protected invention, including activities that are necessary for obtaining an authorization from the competent authority for placing on the market a product which is a drug intended for use on humans or animals, or a medicinal product or plant protection products defined by the Plant Breeders' Rights Act.

123. The doctrine of exhaustion of intellectual property rights applies to patents as well. The exclusive rights conferred by a patent shall not extend to acts relating to a product in which a protected invention is materialized, when the product has been put on the market in the RS by the patent holder or with his consent. The exclusive rights conferred by a patent are also limited in case of a direct, individual preparation of a drug in a pharmacy based on a single prescription, and the placement of such drug on the market.

124. Similarly to limitations of exclusive rights on a design,[51] the Serbian legislator prescribes a limitation of a patent for the purpose of facilitating of the international traffic. Namely, a patent protection cannot be invoked against a person who

50. *Ibid.*, Arts 21–38.
51. *See* Industrial Design Act, Art. 44.

uses devices made on the basis of a protected invention, where such devices constitute an element in the structure or equipment of a vessel, aircraft or land vehicle or which serve exclusively for the operation of such vessel, aircraft or land vehicle belonging to a Member State to the Paris Union or member of the WTO, when such vehicle enters the territory of RS temporarily or accidentally.

125. As already explained, the Serbian legislator opted for the *first to file* system, thus recognizing the right to the grant of a patent for a given invention to the first person to file a patent application, regardless of the date of actual invention. To remedy the deficiencies of the *first to file* system, the Patent Act prescribed the right of a prior user. Namely, a patent has no effect against a person acting in good faith that has, before the date of priority, already started exploiting a protected invention in production in the territory of the RS, or has made all necessary preparations to initiate such use. That person ('a prior user') is entitled to continue exploiting the invention exclusively for production purposes, in its own plant or in the plant of another person for his own needs. The prior user cannot assign the right to exploitation of the invention to another person, except together with the enterprise or part of the enterprise in which the preparation for use or the use of the invention has taken place.[52]

126. The Patent Act prescribes certain limitations of rights concerning biological material as well. By acquiring protected plant propagating material from the patent holder or with his consent, a farmer obtains authorization to use the product of said propagating material for further propagation or multiplication on his own farm, under conditions prescribed by the Plant Breeders' Rights Act. The products obtained in such a manner may not be used for commercial purposes. Similarly, by acquiring protected animal reproductive material or breeding stock from the patent holder or with his consent, a farmer obtains authorization for use protected livestock or for reproductive material for the purpose of his own agricultural activities, but not for sale within the framework or for the purpose of a commercial reproduction activity.

127. Furthermore, the Patent Act limits the exclusive rights of the patent holder by allowing the grant of compulsory licenses. There are several types of compulsory licenses in Serbian patent law. Still, although the legislator regulated the issuance of compulsory licenses in detail, in practice they are almost never granted. So far, only one compulsory licence was granted and this occurred between the two world wars.[53] Under the Patent Act, a compulsory licence may be granted if the patent holder refuses to license the right of commercial use of a protected invention to other person(s) or sets unreasonable conditions for such licensing, provided that:

- the right holder or a person authorized by the right holder does not use the protected invention or uses the protected invention insufficiently in the RS; or

52. *See* Marković, S.: 'Pravo ranijeg korisnika patentiranog pronalaska kao ograničenje patenta: ogled o jednom marginalnom pitanju patentnog prava', in *Pravo i privreda*, n° 7–9/2014, 13–27.
53. *See* Marković, S.: *Patentno pravo*, Nomos, Belgrade, 1997. 310.

- the commercial use of an invention that has been subsequently protected by another person is not possible without the use of the protected invention in whole or in part; or
- it is necessary to remedy a practice determined to be anticompetitive in a judicial or administrative proceedings.

A compulsory licence is granted by the ministry competent in the field in which the invention is employed, at the request of an interested party. The first type of the compulsory licence concerns the cases of non-use of insufficient use of a patented invention in the RS. However, a compulsory licence shall not be granted if the patent holder provides legitimate reasons to justify non-exploitation or insufficiency of exploitation of the protected invention. The second type concerns the cases of interdependent inventions that request cross-licensing. The licence may be granted only if the second invention involves a technical advancement of special economic significance in relation to the first protected invention. The third type of compulsory licenses represents a remedy to anticompetitive behaviour by undertakings which are patent holders. In our opinion, the third category of compulsory licenses is redundant, given the fact that compulsory licensing may be achieved, in less complex and more efficient procedure, before the Serbian Competition Authority (in Serbian, *Komisija za zaštitu konkurencije*), by means of behavioural remedies.[54]

128. The request for the grant of a compulsory licence cannot be filed before the expiration of a period of four years from the date of filing of the patent application or before the expiration of a period of three years from the grant of the patent, whichever period expires last. Before making a request for the grant of a compulsory licence, the interested person must prove that he has made efforts to obtain authorization for the use of the protected invention from the right holder on reasonable commercial terms and that such efforts have not been successful within a reasonable period of time. The person requesting the grant of a compulsory licence must prove that he has the appropriate technological capacity and production facilities for the commercial use of the protected invention. Special rules apply to compulsory licenses granted when the public emergency endangers the survival of the state or its citizens or in cases of public non-commercial use. In these two situations, the party requesting the grant of a compulsory licence need not prove that it attempted to enter into licensing agreement with the patent holder, nor it has to wait for the expiration of a time limit to submit its request.

129. The party in favour of which a compulsory licence is granted is required to pay the patent holder a mutually agreed remuneration. In the absence of an agreement on the amount and method of payment of such remuneration, the licence fee shall be determined by the court. A compulsory licence may be granted only as a non-exclusive one. It may be terminated if and when circumstances that have led to

54. *See* Popović, D.: *Isključiva prava intelektualne svojine i slobodna konkurencija*, Pravni fakultet Univerziteta u Beogradu, Belgrade, 2012, 116–120.

its grant cease to exist and are unlikely to recur. It may be assigned only with the manufacturing plant that exploits the invention for which the licence has been granted.

130. A compulsory licence is predominantly granted for the supply of the domestic market. However, the Patent Act allows for the grant of compulsory licenses relating to the manufacture of pharmaceutical products for export to countries with public health problems. Namely, the Ministry of Health may grant a compulsory licence in relation to patents and supplementary protection certificates (SPCs) concerning the manufacture and sale of pharmaceutical products, when such products are intended for export to importing countries having public health problems to any person who submits a request.[55] When deciding on the grant of a compulsory licence, the Ministry takes into account the need for execution of decisions of the WTO Council on 30 August 2003 on the implementation of item (6) of the Doha Declaration on the Agreement on Trade-Related Aspects of Intellectual Property Rights and Public Health on 14 November 2001. The following countries are eligible for importing countries:

- any least-developed country appearing as such in the United Nations list;
- any member of the WTO, other than the least-developed country members according to the UN list, that has made a notification to the Council for TRIPS of its intention to use the system as an importer; and
- any country that is not a member of the WTO, but is listed in the OECD Development Assistance Committee's list of low-income countries with a gross national product per capita of less than amount established by the OECD Development Assistance Committee, and has made a notification to the Government of its intention to use the system as an importer.

A compulsory licence may only be granted if the interested party provides the evidence that it has made efforts to obtain authorization from the right holder, and that such efforts have not been successful within a period of thirty days before submitting the request. The party in favour of which a compulsory licence is granted is required to pay the patent holder a licence fee:

- in the cases of national emergency or other circumstances of extreme urgency or in cases of public non-commercial use, the remuneration shall be a maximum of 4% of the total price to be paid by the importing country or on its behalf;
- in all other cases, the remuneration shall be determined taking into account the economic value of the use authorized under the licence to the importing country or countries concerned, as well as humanitarian and non-commercial circumstances relating to the grant of the licence.

55. Popović, D.: 'Usklađivanje patentnog prava Republike Srbije sa međunarodnopravnim standardima zaštite pronalazaka', in V. Radović ed., *Usklađivanje poslovnog prava Srbije sa pravom Evropske unije (2012)*, Pravni fakultet Univerziteta u Beogradu, Beograd, 2012, 281–303.

131. Finally, the Patent Act prescribed a specific type of compulsory licence aiming at remedying the inter-dependence of certain patented inventions and protected plant varieties. Such compulsory licence may be granted in two cases. First, where a plant breeder cannot obtain or exploit a plant breeder's right without infringing a prior patent concerning a biotechnological invention, he may file the request for the grant of a compulsory licence to the Ministry of Agriculture for the use of the invention protected by the patent. Second, where the holder of a patent concerning a biotechnological invention cannot exploit it without infringing a prior plant breeders' right, it may file the request for the grant of a compulsory licence to the Ministry of Agriculture. Such licence may not be exclusive. If such a licence is granted, the holder of the plant breeders' right will be entitled to a cross-licence.

§8. Duration of Protection

132. An invention which meets the patentability requirements prescribed by the Patent Act is protected, upon registration by the IP Office, for a period of twenty years as of from the date of the filing of the application.[56] However, a patent shall cease if the right owner fails to renew its right, i.e., fails to pay the prescribed fee for maintenance of the right. If the right holder fails to pay the fee, the latter may be validly paid within an additional time period of six months, provided a prescribed additional fee is paid at the same time. A patent shall also cease in the following cases:

- if a patent holder relinquishes his right, on the day following the day on which the IP Office receives the statement of relinquishment;[57]
- if the legal person has been dissolved, or if the natural person who is the right holder has deceased, on the day of dissolution of the legal person, or death of natural person, unless a patent has been transferred to legal successors of such persons.

133. The IP Office may revoke at any time the decision to grant a patent, in whole or in part, on the request of any interested person, if it establishes that:

- the subject matter of protection is not an invention within the meaning of the Patent Act;
- the invention falls under the category of inventions excluded from protection;
- the invention was not new on the date of the filing of the patent application or on the date of priority, or did not involve an inventive step or was not industrially applicable;
- the invention is not disclosed in a manner sufficiently clear and complete as defined by the Patent Act;

56. *See* Patent Act, Art. 39.
57. However, if any right on the patent belonging to a third party has been entered into the Registry, the patent holder cannot waive its right without a prior written consent from the party owning such right (e.g., license, pledge).

– the scope of rights granted exceeds the scope that could be supported by the description of the invention as disclosed on the filing date or priority date of the application, or if protection was granted on a divisional application, the subject matter of which extends beyond the basic application as filed.

A decision to revoke the patent in part or in whole does not produce any effect on court decisions on infringement of rights, which were legally binding at the moment of the adoption of the decision revoking the patent, nor on assignment and licensing agreements that have been entered into, if, and to the extent that, such agreements have been executed, provided the plaintiff and patent holder have acted in good faith.

134. Certain products which represent a materialization of an invention may be protected by an SPC following the termination of a patent. This type of protection concerns a product, not an invention itself. SPC applies to specific pharmaceutical and plant protection products that have been authorized by regulatory authorities. SPCs aim to offset the loss of patent protection for pharmaceutical and plant protection products that occurs due to the compulsory lengthy testing and clinical trials these products require prior to obtaining regulatory marketing approval. The marketing approval is delivered by the Medical and Medical Devices Agency (ALIMS) or the Ministry of Agriculture, depending on the type of product concerned. The SPC takes effect at the end of the lawful term of the basic patent. Duration of protection for granted SPC is equal to the period which elapsed between the date on which the application for a basic patent was lodged and the date of the first authorization to place the product on the market, reduced by a period of five years. The duration of the certificate may not exceed five years from the date on which it takes effect.

§9. Infringement and Remedies

135. Patent infringements are subject to civil and criminal remedies. Civil remedies are regulated under the Patent Act as *lex specialis*,[58] with the subsidiary application of general rules on civil procedure and rules on the assessment of damages. A patent infringement consists in any unauthorized use of a protected invention in production, placing on the market of products made by the protected invention, disposing of the patent, or in undertaking any other activity which falls within the scope of the exclusive rights without the consent of a right holder. The complaint on the grounds of infringement of a patent may be filed by the patent holder, the acquirer of exclusive licence or the patent applicant. The applicant and the acquirer of the exclusive licence are entitled to infringement action upon the publication of the patent application. In case of joint ownership of a patent or in case of a joint patent application, each co-owner/co-applicant is entitled to initiate infringement proceedings in its own name and on its own behalf.

58. *See* Patent Act, Arts 132–144.

136. The complaint for patent infringement may be filed within three years following the day the plaintiff has become aware of the infringement and the infringer, but not later than within five years following the day when infringement was committed (or following the day when infringement was last committed, in case of continuous infringements). The plaintiff may request, *inter alia*:

- that infringement of the right be determined;
- cessation of the infringement of right;
- that the articles used in infringement of the right be destroyed or modified;
- that the tools and equipment used for production of the articles used in infringement of the right be destroyed or modified, if that is necessary for the efficient protection of the right;
- compensation for material damages and reasonable costs of procedure;
- information on any third persons participating in infringement of the right to be revealed;
- publishing of the wording of the court decision in the media.

137. The person infringing a patent is held liable for the injury pursuant to the general rules on compensation of damages. The court may, in appropriate cases, adjudge to the injured party the compensation as a lump sum which cannot not be lower than the licence remuneration for particular use of the protected subject matter.

138. The court may order an interim measure at the request of the person who makes it credible that the patent or the right arising from the application has been infringed, or that such infringement is imminent. The interim measure may consist in the seizure or withdrawal from circulation of the articles used in infringement, or the measure of prohibiting continuation of any activities by way of which the infringement may be/is committed. Further to this type of interim measure, the court may also comply with the request of the person who makes it credible that the patent or the right arising from the application has been infringed, or that such infringement is imminent, or that irreparable harm is likely to occur, or that there is a reasonable suspicion that evidence will be destroyed or that it will not be possible to collect it later, to order an interim measure to secure evidence without giving prior notice to, or hearing the person from whom the evidence is to be collected. The securing of evidence is being realized through the inspection of premises, vehicles, books, documents, as well as the seizure of documents and infringing goods, questioning of witnesses and expert witnesses. Both types of measures may be requested even before filing a complaint, provided that subsequently a complaint is filed within thirty days from the date of rendering the decision on interim measure/on securing the evidence.

139. The Patent Act prescribes that the provisions of the Civil Procedure Act[59] and the Enforcement Act[60] are to be applied by analogy. Also, damages-related claims should be resolved by analogous application of provisions of the Contract and Torts Act.[61]

140. Further to civil law remedies, the Patent Act lists certain types of conduct that are subject to (pseudo)criminal penalties.[62] Namely, a legal person who has infringed a patent or a right arising from the registration application is sanctioned on grounds of corporate offence (in Serbian, *privredni prestup*) by a fine. A responsible person in a legal entity who is found to infringe a patent may also be fined. The infringing objects and the objects used for the perpetration of the corporate offence may be forfeited and the infringing objects may be destroyed. An entrepreneur or a natural person who has infringed a patent or a right arising from the registration application is sanctioned on grounds of misdemeanour by a fine. The infringing objects in a misdemeanour and the objects used for perpetration of the misdemeanour may be forfeited and the infringing objects may be destroyed. Finally, a natural or legal person who acts as representative in the exercising of the rights under the Patent Act without a power of attorney is sanctioned on grounds of misdemeanour by a fine. The responsible person in a legal entity may also be fined.

§10. Overlapping and Relation to Other Intellectual Property Rights

141. Inventions relating to the structure of a product or the layout of its components may be protected by petty patent.[63] Such protection is often sought for innovations of a rather incremental character. The applicant may file a request for the conversion of the petty patent application into patent application and vice versa, prior to the adoption of a decision to grant a right. A converted application retains the filing date of the application for a petty patent or of the originally filed application.[64]

142. As explained *supra*, by acquiring protected plant propagating material from the patent holder or with his consent, a farmer obtains authorization to use the product of said propagating material for further propagation or multiplication on his own farm, under conditions prescribed by the Plant Breeders' Rights Act. The products obtained in such a manner may not be used for commercial purposes.[65]

---

59. Official Journal of the Republic of Serbia, n° 72/2011, 49/2013, 74/2013, 55/2014, 87/2018 and 18/2020.
60. *Ibid.*, n° 106/2015, 106/2016, 113/2017 and 54/2019.
61. Official Journal of the SFR Yugoslavia, n° 29/78, 39/85, 45/89; Official Journal of the FR Yugoslavia, n° 31/93; Official Journal of the Union of Serbia and Montenegro, n° 1/2003; Official Journal of the Republic of Serbia, n° 18/2020.
62. *See* Patent Act, Arts 170–171.
63. *See* Ch. 3.
64. *See* Patent Act, Art. 166.
65. *Ibid.*, Art. 25.

Chapter 3. Petty Patents

§1. Sources – Legislation

143. In Serbian intellectual property law, petty patents are regulated under the Patent Act.[66] With respect to the registration procedure, the Government of Serbia adopted the Regulation on the contents of the registry of applications and the registry of patents, the mandatory elements of applications for a patent registration, and the data published in the Official Journal of the IP Office (hereinafter, the Regulation).[67] The National Registry of Petty Patents is available on the website of the IP Office.[68]

§2. The Protection of Inventions by Petty Patents

144. Up until the adoption of the 2011 Patent Act, the prescribed inventive level for petty patents was lower than the one required for patent protection. However, the patentability criteria are presently the same regardless of the type of patent protection sought. Therefore, petty patents may be granted for inventions that are new, involve an inventive step and are susceptible of industrial application. This abandonment of the concept of petty patents as an instrument of protection for inventions of a lower inventive level was criticized in legal theory.[69] Not all inventions may be protected by a petty patent. Only a solution relating to the structure of a product or the layout of its components may be the subject matter of an invention protected by petty patent.

145. Petty patents are recognized in proceedings before the IP Office. The proceedings are initiated by way of submitting a petty patent application. A petty patent application may contain only one independent claim and maximum four dependent claims. A petty patent application can be divided into two or more independent applications (divisional application). It cannot be filed as the application for patent of addition. Unlike a patent application, a petty patent application is not published in the Official Journal of the IP Office. If the IP Office finds that a petty patent application meets the formal requirements prescribed by the Patent Act, it shall grant a petty patent. Once a registration fee is paid, a decision on the grant of petty patent shall be published in the Official Journal of the IP Office.

66. Official Journal of the Republic of Serbia, n° 99/2011, Arts 163–167.
67. *Ibid.*, n° 113/2012.
68. The Registry is available at: *http://www.zis.gov.rs* .
69. *See* Marković, S.: 'Mali patent u patentnom pravu Srbije', in B. Vlašković ed., *Pravne i infrastrukturne osnove za razvoj ekonomije zasnovane na znanju (2013),* Pravni fakultet Univerziteta u Kragujevcu, Kragujevac, 2013, 65–77; Popović, D.: 'Usklađivanje patentnog prava Republike Srbije sa međunarodnopravnim standardima zaštite pronalazaka', in V. Radović ed., *Usklađivanje poslovnog prava Srbije sa pravom Evropske unije (2012),* Pravni fakultet Univerziteta u Beogradu, Beograd, 2012, 281–303.

146. At any moment prior to the decision to grant a petty patent, the applicant may file a request for the conversion of a petty patent application into patent application or industrial design application, and vice versa. A converted application shall retain the filing date of the application for a petty patent or of the originally filed application.

147. In the course of the proceedings, the IP Office shall not examine whether the invention meets the substantive criteria: novelty, inventive step and industrial applicability. However, once a petty patent granted, the right holder may request the IP Office to examine these substantive criteria. If the requirements are met, the IP Office shall issue to the petty patent holder the certificate of examination. If the requirements are not met, the IP Office shall ex officio revoke the petty patent. A notification of the issued certificate of examination and a decision on revocation of petty patent are published in the Official Journal of the IP Office and entered into the Registry of petty patents. In case of a petty patent infringement, the right holder can initiate civil law proceedings before a competent court only if it proves that the IP Office had successfully conducted substantive requirements examination. Therefore, the examination of patentability criteria is a pre-requirement for the civil law protection of a petty patent.

Chapter 4. Trademarks

§1. Source – Legislation

148. The tradition of trademark protection in Serbia is a long-standing one. The Kingdom of Serbia adopted its first Trademark Act in 1884, almost half a century prior to the adoption of its first patent rules, in 1920. At the time, Serbia actively participated in European trade in goods, while the industry was only starting to develop. These characteristics of the national economy lead to the early adoption of trademark and design protection rules, while the protection of inventions needed not be regulated in a short run. The development of trademark law and of the intellectual property law in general stagnated during the country's socialist period following World War II. However, by the end of the twentieth century, Serbia became party to all major international trademark conventions. The SFR of Yugoslavia, which Serbia was a part of, ratified the Madrid agreement concerning the international registration of marks (1891).[70] The Federal Republic of Yugoslavia, which Serbia was a part of, ratified the Protocol to the Madrid agreement (1989),[71] the Nairobi treaty on the protection of the Olympic symbol (1981),[72] the Trademark law treaty (1994).[73] Following the complete disintegration of Yugoslavia, Serbia, as an independent country, ratified the Vienna Agreement establishing an international classification of the figurative elements of marks (1973),[74] the Nice Agreement concerning the international classification of goods and services for the purposes of the registration of marks (1957)[75] and the Singapore Treaty on the law of trademarks (2006).[76] Since Serbia is currently negotiating its accession to the WTO and the European Union, the national trademark rules are harmonized not only with the previously mentioned international conventions, but also with the TRIPS and the sources of EU law.

149. Contemporary Serbian trademark law is governed by the Trademark Act, adopted in 2020.[77] With respect to the registration procedure, the Government of Serbia adopted Regulation on the contents of the registry of applications and the registry of trademarks, the mandatory elements of applications for a trademark registration, and the data published in the Official Journal of the IP Office (hereinafter, the Regulation).[78]

---

70. Official Journal of the SFR Yugoslavia – International Agreements, n° 2/1974.
71. Official Journal of the FR Yugoslavia – International Agreements, n° 2/1997.
72. *Ibid.*, n° 1/1999.
73. *Ibid.*, n° 4/1998.
74. Official Journal of the Republic of Serbia – International Agreements, n° 42/2009.
75. *Ibid.*, n° 19/2010.
76. *Ibid.*, n° 5/2010.
77. Official Journal of the Republic of Serbia, n° 6/2020.
78. *Ibid.*, n° 25/2021.

150. Finally, the IP Office adopted its Methodological guidebook on trademark registration and other proceedings before the Office, which is available on its website.[79]

§2. SUBJECT MATTER OF PROTECTION

I. Signs Which May Serve as Trademarks

151. Under the Trademark Act, any sign suitable for distinguishing in the course of trade the goods or services of one natural or legal person from the goods or services of another natural or legal person may be protected as a trademark. The legislator enumerated *exempli causa* several signs that in principle may be registered as trademarks: words, slogans, letters, numbers, images, drawings, combinations of colours, three-dimensional shapes, combinations of such signs, as well as sounds.

152. Words may be registered as trademarks, provided they are not generic terms, i.e., an indicator of the entire category of goods or services. A combination of letters, not necessarily forming an existing word, may be registered as a trademark, provided it is distinctive. The criterion of distinctiveness applies to other types of signs as well, including the combinations of numbers or slogans. Graphical representations, be they drawings or images, may also serve as trademarks, independently or in combination with verbal signs. However, signs which are contrary to public policy or to accepted principles of morality cannot be protected as a trademark.[80]

153. Personal names are generally admitted as trademarks. The name or portrait of a person may be protected as a trademark only with a person's consent. If such person is deceased, a trademark may be registered only with consent of parents, spouse and children of a deceased person. The name or portrait of a historical or other famous but deceased person may be registered as a trademark only with the authorization of the competent authority (e.g., a cultural heritage foundation) and the consent of the deceased person's relatives up to the third degree of kinship.[81] However, the trademark owner may not prevent others from using, in accordance with good business practices, of their name or address.[82]

154. Exceptionally, three-dimensional shapes may be registered as trademarks, if an average consumer associates the very form of a product to a certain producer/ product. The 3D trademarks are rarely admitted, as their generalization would otherwise devoid a design protection of its purpose. Musical phrases may be registered

79. The Methodological guidebook is available at: *http://www.zis.gov.rs* .
80. *See* Trademark Act, Art. 5.
81. *Ibid.*
82. *Ibid.*, Art. 54.

as trademarks, provided they could be graphically represented. The protection of musical phrases by trademark right may overlap with a copyright protection of music works.

155. Further to the prohibition of registration of signs which are contrary to public policy and/or accepted principles of morality, the Trademark Act prescribes other grounds for refusal of trademark protection. Under Article 5 of the Act, a trademark shall not be used to protect a sign which has a general appearance that does not enable goods or services to be distinguished in the course of trade. For example, the IP Office refused to register a descriptive sign 'The leading small hotels of the world' for lack of distinctiveness.[83] Also, a sign which consists exclusively of the shape which results from the nature of the goods themselves, or the shape of goods which is necessary to obtain a technical result, or the shape which gives substantial value to the goods, cannot be registered. A trademark protection shall also be refused to signs which consist exclusively of indications that may serve, in the course of trade, to designate the kind, quality, quantity, intended purpose, value, geographical origin, or the time of production of the goods or of rendering of the service, or other characteristics of goods or services. Furthermore, a sign which has become customary in the current language or in the bona fide and established practices of trade cannot be registered as a trademark. A sign which contains hallmarks of quality control or warranty, or imitations thereof, cannot be registered either. For example, the IP Office refused to register a sign 'ISO sport', since it partly consists of an indication used as a hallmark of quality control (ISO standards).[84]

156. A sign that consists of state or other public coat of arms, flag or other emblem, name or abbreviation of the name of a country or of an international organization, or imitations thereof, cannot be registered as a trademark, unless the competent authority or the country or organization concerned has given its authorization for such use. Further to this, a sign which represents or imitates a national or religious symbol cannot be registered as a trademark. For example, the IP Office refused to grant protection to the sign being a representation of one of the most famous frescoes of the Serbian Orthodox Church entitled 'Beli andjeo' ('White angel'), although the trademark application was submitted by the monastery in which the fresco is painted.[85] The IP Office considered that the 'White angel' is not only an art masterpiece but also a religious symbol.

157. Certain signs, although they meet the criterion of distinctiveness, may not be registered as a trademark if they are likely, due to their representation or content, to deceive the public, for instance, as to the nature, quality or geographical origin of the goods or services. For example, the IP Office refused to register a sign 'Le coq' (in French, rooster) for a category of products relating to meat, fish and oil.[86] The

83. Trademark application nº Z-1999-0731, 18 Nov. 1999.
84. Trademark application nº Z-878/01, 8 Jun. 2001.
85. Trademark application nº Z-2003-1728, 29 Dec. 2003.
86. Trademark application nº IR 678849, 24 Sep. 1998.

IP Office considered that such a sign was capable of deceiving the average consumers as to the nature of the goods. Once the applicant submitted a limited list of products for which the registration is claimed, the trademark was registered. Similarly, the IP Office refused to grant protection to the sign 'French connection' for products such as perfumes, make-up and handbags made in Serbia. The IP Office considered that an average consumer would be deceived as to the origin of the product (an average consumer would wrongfully believe that the goods originate in France and not in Serbia), as well as to the quality of the products (France is particularly famous as a producer of high-quality products in these categories).[87]

158. If a sign, by its appearance or content, is identical or similar to an intellectual good protected by copyright or industrial property right owned by a third party, its registration shall be refused. A possible infringement of an industrial property right may be determined by a simple verification of rights' databases administered by the IP Office. However, a potential copyright infringement may not be determined in such a way. If the IP Office proceeds with a trademark registration, a copyright owner may initiate annulment proceedings.

159. As is the case in comparative and international trademark law, Serbian trademark law is also governed by the principle of speciality. Therefore, a sign that is identical with a protected trademark already registered for identical category of goods or services shall not be granted protection. Furthermore, a sign which is identical to an earlier protected trademark of another person for similar type of goods or services, or which is similar to an earlier protected trademark of another person for identical or similar type of goods or services, if such identity and/or similarity is likely to cause confusion in the relevant part of the public, including the likelihood of association with the earlier protected trademark, shall not be registered. The Trademark Act prescribes an exception to the speciality principle with respect to well-known trademarks. Namely, a sign which is identical or similar to a sign of another person for identical or similar goods or services, which is well known in Serbia within the meaning of Article 6*bis* of the Paris Convention, shall not be registered. In establishing whether a sign is well known, the familiarity of the relevant part of the public with the trademark shall be taken into account, including their familiarity with the trademark as a consequence of promotional activities in respect of the trademark. The relevant part of the public is to be understood as the actual or potential users of the goods or services designated by the trademark, as well as the persons involved in the process of distribution of the respective goods or services. However, the registration would be granted if the trademark owner provided a written consent.

160. Finally, a sign which represents an imitation, reproduction, transliteration or transcription of a registered trademark of another person, or the essential segment thereof, which is known to market participants as a sign of widespread reputation (famous trademark), may not be registered as a trademark, if the use of such a sign would result in unfair advantage from the reputation acquired by the famous

87. Trademark application n° Z-0023/04, 13 Jan. 2004.

trademark or in harm to its distinctive character and/or reputation. However, the owner of a famous trademark may consent to such a registration.

II. Different Categories of Trademarks

161. The Trademark Act differentiates among three categories of trademarks: individual, collective and certification trademarks.[88] A collective trademark is a trademark owned by a legal person representing an association of manufacturers and/or service providers, which may be used by the members of association under the conditions prescribed by the Trademark Act and the General Act on Collective Trademark. The owner of a collective trademark is entitled to use the registered sign in parallel with the members of association. On the other hand, a certification trademark is a trademark used by several legal persons under supervision of the trademark holder. The registered sign serves as a guaranty of quality, geographic origin, manner of manufacturing or other common characteristics of the goods and/or services provided by such legal persons. The owner of a certification trademark is usually not a producer/service provider, but only a supervisor of the use of a registered sign. The owner of a certification trademark has to allow any company to use the registered sign for goods and/or services which have common characteristics prescribed by the General Act on Certification Trademark.

§3. Conditions of Protection

162. In order to be protected, a trademark must meet both positive and negative requirements. As already explained, under the Trademark Act only distinctive signs may be registered as trademarks. Distinctiveness is defined as a capacity of a sign to distinguish the goods and/or services in the course of trade. Furthermore, a sign must not be contrary to public order or morality, must not infringe intellectual property rights of other persons, must not contain state or any other public coat of arms, flag or emblem, name or abbreviated name of a country or an international organization, religious or national symbols, as well as imitations thereof, except under the consent by the competent authority, nor it could reproduce or imitate a well-known sign.[89] Some of these requirements are qualified in the Trademark Act as ‘absolute grounds for refusal of protection’ while others are qualified as ‘relative grounds for refusal of protection’. The IP Office verifies *ex officio* the existence of absolute and relative grounds for refusal, while the owners of prior rights may initiate opposition procedure only in case they consider that the relative grounds for refusal of trademark protection are met.

---

88. *See* Trademark Act, Art. 2.
89. *Ibid.*, Arts 4–6.

§4. Formalities: Procedure for Obtaining Protection

163. Protection of trademarks is obtained by means of registration before the IP Office of the RS. Unregistered trademarks are not protected under the Trademark Act, but may enjoy protection under the Unfair Competition Act.

I. Application for a Trademark Registration

164. The procedure before the IP Office is initiated by filling an application for a trademark registration. A trademark right is vested in a person who created or chose a certain sign and submitted an application, or in his legal successor, or in the employer in specific cases prescribed by the law. Foreign natural and legal persons enjoy the national treatment if it results from international agreements or under reciprocity principle. A party invoking reciprocity between Serbia and a foreign country is supposed to submit the proof of its existence. Foreign natural and legal persons who have no residence or seat in Serbia must be represented by a local attorney or agent registered within the IP Office.[90]

165. A written application for a trademark registration is to be submitted to the IP Office in person or by post. The mandatory elements of the application are:

- request for the protection of a trademark;
- reproduction of a sign for which the protection is requested; and
- indication of a category of goods/services to which the sign relates (in accordance with the Nice Agreement Classification).

One trademark may be registered for goods/services belonging to several categories, which is commonly the case. The request for a trademark registration must contain:

- applicant's personal data; and
- indication of the type of trademark for which the request is submitted: individual, collective or certification trademark.

If a sign for which the application for a trademark registration is submitted contains a figurative element, the depiction of such element has to be clear, made on a good quality paper and suitable for reproduction.

166. In addition to the before-mentioned documents, an applicant for a collective or certification trademark registration has to submit a General Act on Collective/Certification Trademark. The General Act on Collective Trademark must contain the particulars of the applicant or its representative, the provisions regarding the appearance of a sign and goods/services to which it relates, the provisions identifying the holders of the right to use a collective trademark and setting out the

90. *See,* Trademark Act, Art. 12.

conditions for such use, the provisions on the rights and obligations of users of the collective trademark in the event of its infringement, and the provisions setting out measures and consequences in case of violation of the provisions of the General Act. The General Act on Certification Trademark has to contain, in addition to these elements, the provisions on common characteristics of goods/services guaranteed by the certification trademark and provisions on the supervision of use of the certification trademark by its holder.[91] Any modification of the General Act has to be notified to the IP Office.

167. Once the application for a trademark registration is submitted and the procedural fees are paid, the IP Office examines the fulfilment of the formal requirements prescribed by the law. From the date of filling the application, the applicant shall enjoy a priority right. An international right of priority is recognized to natural and legal persons who filed an industrial design right application in any Member State of the Paris Union or the WTO within the timeframe of six months preceding the filing of application in Serbia. An exhibition priority right is recognized to applicants that used a sign to mark a product/service at a national fair or international exhibition or in any other state of the Paris Union or the WTO within three months preceding the date of filing of the application before the Serbian IP Office.[92]

II. Grant of a Trademark Right

168. If the formal requirements that a trademark application must satisfy have been fulfilled, the IP Office shall proceed to examining the fulfilment of substantive requirements.[93]

Where the application was found to meet the criterion of distinctiveness and other registration requirements (both 'absolute' and 'relative conditions'), the IP Office shall issue a decision requesting the applicant to pay the registration fee for the first ten years of protection, as well as the costs of publication of a trademark, and submit the proof of payments made. Once the proof of payments is submitted, the IP Office shall issue the decision on the registration of a trademark, which will subsequently be entered into the Trademark Registry. The holder of a trademark right shall be issued a trademark right certificate. The grant of a trademark right is published in the Official Journal of the IP Office.

169. However, if the IP Office establishes that the application does not meet the registration requirements, it shall notify the applicant in writing of the reasons due to which a trademark right cannot be granted and invite the applicant to submit its observations. Where the applicant fails to respond, or where the applicant responds but the IP Office nevertheless considers that a trademark may not be registered, a decision on refusal of a trademark registration shall be issued. The refusal may be partial, e.g., the IP Office may decide not to register a trademark in all categories of

91. *Ibid.*, Art. 16.
92. *Ibid.*, Arts 19–23.
93. *Ibid.*, Arts 30–39.

goods/services for which a request was submitted. A special procedure is prescribed in case a sign for which the trademark protection is requested comprises the elements which are descriptive, necessary or customary. If that is the case, the IP Office may request the applicant to submit a written statement disclaiming any exclusive rights in respect of such an element. Once a 'disclaimer' is submitted, the IP Office may decide to proceed with the registration of a trademark. The 2020 Trademark Act introduced into Serbian trademark law the 'opposition procedure' modelled upon European trademark law. The opposition procedure may be initiated by owners of prior rights which consider that one or more relative grounds for refusal of trademark protection are present in case at hand.[94] The opposition procedure may also be initiated by a company whose business name, registered before the date of filing of a trademark application or before the date of priority, is identical or similar to the sign for which the trademark application has been submitted to the IP Office.[95]

170. If a request for collective or certification trademark registration is submitted, the IP Office shall examine whether the General Act on Collective/Certification Trademark is in contravention of the public policy or the accepted principles of morality. This examination shall be repeated each time the General Act is modified.

§5. Ownership and Transfer: Assignment – Licenses

171. The owner of a trademark right is a natural or legal person who submitted a trademark registration request which was consequently approved. The particulars of the right owner are entered into the Trademark Register, administered by the IP Office. Ownership of the rights with regard to trademarks created in the employment context (e.g., under instructions received from an employer) is regulated by analogy to ownership of patents on inventions created by an employee.

172. The rights granted with regard to a registered trademark may be assigned. Assignment of a trademark right and/or right arising from a trademark application may result from the assignment agreement, change of status of the holder of a trademark right and/or the applicant, or a court or administrative decision. Assignment is to be recorded in the appropriate registry of the IP Office. Registration of the assignment produces effects with respect to third parties. In case the assignment results from an assignment agreement, such an agreement must be concluded in written form and contain a designation of contracting parties, the indication of the category of goods/services to which a trademark relates, and the amount of remuneration, if stipulated. Collective trademarks and certification trademarks may not be subject to assignment.[96]

---

94. *Ibid.,* Arts 34–37.
95. *Ibid.,* Art. 7.
96. *See* Trademark Act, Arts 63–64, 68–70. General rules on contractual transfer of rights laid down by the Contract and Torts Act are also applicable.

173. The trademark owner and/or the applicant may grant licence with respect to the right to use the registered trademark and/or trademark for which the registration application is submitted, in respect of all or some of the goods/services, by entering into a licensing agreement. The agreement has to be concluded in writing and contain indication of the contracting parties, trademark registration number or registration application number, the term of validity of the licence and the scope of the licence. The licence agreement is to be recorded in the appropriate registry of the IP Office. Registration of the licence agreement produces effects with respect to third parties. Collective trademarks and certification trademarks may not be subject to a licence agreement.[97]

174. The rights granted with regard to trademark may be pledged. The trademark owner and/or the applicant may pledge the trademark right and/or right arising from the trademark registration application, with respect of all or some of the goods/services, by entering into an agreement of pledge. The agreement has to be concluded in written form and is to be recorded in the appropriate registry of the IP Office. Pledge may also result from a court or administrative decision. Collective trademarks and certification trademarks may not be subject of pledge.[98]

§6. Scope of Exclusive Rights

175. A registered trademark confers to its holder the exclusive right to use it and to prevent any third party not having his consent from using it.[99] The aforementioned use covers, in particular:

- the act of affixing the protected trademark to the goods, the packaging for the goods or labelling instruments (labels, stickers, bottle stoppers, and the like);
- offering of goods, their placement into circulation or storage for such purposes, or supply of services under the protected trademark;
- import, export or transit of the goods under the protected trademark; and
- using the protected trademark in business documentation or in advertisements.

A trademark owner is entitled to prohibit other persons from illicitly using a trademark identical to an earlier protected mark of the trademark owner for goods/services which are identical to the goods/services the trademark is registered for. The trademark owner is also entitled to prohibit other persons from illicitly using a trademark identical to an earlier protected trademark of the trademark owner for a similar category of goods/services, or a trademark which is similar to the trademark owner's earlier protected trademark for identical or similar category of goods/ services, if there is a likelihood of confusion among the relevant segment of the public

97. *See* Trademark Act, Arts 65–66. General rules on license agreements laid down by the Contract and Torts Act are also applicable.
98. *See* Trademark Act, Art. 67. General rules on pledge of movable assets and rights are also applicable.
99. *See* Trademark Act, Art. 49.

due to such identicalness and/or similarity, including the likelihood of association of that trademark with the trademark owner's earlier protected trademark.

176. The Trademark Act laid down a special rule applicable in case a reproduction of a protected trademark in a dictionary, encyclopaedia or similar publication creates an impression that the trademark is a generic term for goods/services for which that trademark has been protected. In such a situation, a trademark owner may request from the publisher that in the following edition, at the latest, the reproduction of the trademark is accompanied by a statement clarifying that the reproduced sign (word) is a protected trademark (followed by the symbol '®').

§7. Exceptions and Limitations to Trademark Protection

177. The Trademark Act prescribes several limitations to exclusive protection of a registered trademark.[100] Namely, a trademark owner cannot prohibit others from placing into circulation their goods/services marked with the same or similar trademark, if that trademark represents their company name or a designation acquired in good faith before the recognized priority date of trademark. Further to this, a trademark owner cannot prohibit others from using, in accordance with good business practices, their name or address, the indication of the type, quality, quantity, purpose, value, geographical origin, date of production or other characteristics of the goods and/or services, or the registered trademark in cases where its use is necessary to indicate the purpose of the goods or services, in particular where the spare parts or equipment are concerned.

178. A trademark owner cannot prohibit others from using the same or similar sign for marking goods/services of a different type (category), except in the case of a well-known trademark. The owner of a registered famous trademark may prevent all third parties not having his consent from using the same or similar sign for marking goods/services, which are not similar to those for which the trademark has been registered if such use of that sign without due cause takes unfair advantage of, or is detrimental to, the distinctive character or the repute of the trademark.

179. The doctrine of exhaustion of intellectual property rights applies to trademark rights as well. The rights conferred by a registered trademark shall not extend to acts relating to a product labelled with such a trademark, when the product has been put on the market by the trademark owner or with his consent. However, the exhaustion rule shall not apply if a trademark owner has a legitimate interest to oppose further placement in circulation of goods marked with such trademark, especially if a defect or other fundamental change of condition of the goods has occurred after their placement into circulation for the first time.

180. Finally, if the object of protection of a collective trademark or certification trademark is a sign that implies a specific geographical area where the goods/

100. *Ibid.*, Arts 53–55.

services originated from, the user of a collective trademark or certification trademark shall not bar others from using such mark in accordance with good business practices or prohibit its use to users of identical or similar indication of geographical origin for the same or similar types of goods/services.

§8. Duration of Protection

181. A trademark which meets the requirements prescribed by the Trademark Act is protected, upon registration by the IP Office, for a period of ten years as of from the date of the filing of the application. The right holder may have the term of protection renewed indefinitely, upon filing a request and payment of the prescribed fee. The request for protection renewal must specify the trademark registration number and the date of lapse of the trademark, particulars of the trademark owner and proof of payment of the prescribed fee.

182. A trademark right shall cease if the right owner fails to renew its right, i.e., fails to pay the prescribed fee for maintenance of the right. However, if a licence, pledge or other right has been entered in the Trademark Register on behalf of a third party, the competent authority shall notify such third party that the fee has not been paid and that it may maintain the validity of the trademark by payment of such fee within a period of six months as of the day it was served such notification.

183. A trademark right shall also cease in the following cases:

- if a trademark owner relinquishes his trademark right, on the day following the day on which the IP Office receives the statement of relinquishment;
- as a result of a court or administrative decision, on the day specified in the concerned decision;
- if the legal person has been dissolved, or if the natural person who is the right holder has deceased, on the day of dissolution of the legal person, or death of natural person, unless a trademark right has been transferred to legal successors of such persons;
- a collective trademark and a certification trademark right shall be terminated if the IP Office, while inspecting the modifications of the General Act on the Collective/Certification Trademark determines that the latter is in contravention of the public policy or the accepted principles of morality.[101]

184. Since the Trademark Act prescribes the duty of a trademark owner to use its registered trademark,[102] the IP Office may issue a decision on revocation of a trademark if the trademark owner or a person authorized by him fails, without a justified reason, to seriously use a trademark on the domestic market for marking of

101. *Ibid.*, Art. 72.
102. *Ibid.*, Art. 59.

goods/services comprised, for an uninterrupted period of five years as of the day on which the trademark was entered in the Trademark Register or from the day of its last use.[103]

185. The IP Office may, at the request of an interested party, issue a decision on revocation of a trademark right in the following cases:

- if the sign protected by a trademark, due to actions or omissions by the trademark owner or his successor in rights, has become a generic term for the goods/services for which it was registered;
- if the sign protected by a trademark right, due to the manner of use by its owner or his successor in rights, has become capable of causing confusion in commerce about the geographical origin, type, quality or other characteristics of the goods/services;
- if the sign protected by a trademark right has become contrary to public policy or to accepted principles of morality;
- if a collective trademark or a certification trademark are being used contrary to the General Act on Collective/Certification Trademark.[104]

186. Finally, the IP Office may declare a trademark registration invalid in whole or for some goods/services comprised, if it is determined that, at the time of issuance of the decision, the requirements for trademark registration prescribed by the Trademark Act have not been met.[105]

§9. Infringement and Remedies

187. Infringements of the exclusive rights on a trademark are subject to civil and criminal remedies. Both types of remedies are regulated under the Trademark Act, with the subsidiary application of general rules on civil and criminal procedure, and rules on the assessment of damages.

188. Civil law remedies are primarily regulated by the Trademark Act. A trademark infringement consists of any unauthorized use of a registered trademark or the sign applied for registration by any economic operator. The imitation of a trademark or the sign applied for registration shall also constitute an infringement. The use of words 'type', 'manner', 'according to the procedure' or a like, along with a protected trademark or a sign applied for registration is also considered to be an infringement. The complaint on the grounds of infringement of a trademark may be filed by the applicant, trademark holder, any user of a collective trademark with the consent of the collective trademark holder, any user of a certification trademark with the consent of the certification trademark holder, and the acquirer of exclusive licence. The latter may file a complaint if the exclusive licence agreement does not

103. *Ibid.*, Arts 82–83.
104. *Ibid.*, Arts 84–85.
105. *Ibid.*, Arts 74–81.

stipulate the contrary. The complaint for trademark infringement may be filed within three years following the day the plaintiff has become aware of the infringement and the infringer, but not later than within five years following the day when infringement was committed for the first time. In case of a trademark infringement, the plaintiff may request, *inter alia*:

- that infringement of the right be determined;
- cessation of the infringement of right;
- that the articles used in infringement of the right be destroyed or modified;
- that the tools and equipment used for production of the articles used in infringement of the right be destroyed or modified, if that is necessary for the efficient protection of the right;
- compensation for material damages and reasonable costs of procedure;
- information on any third persons participating in infringement of the right to be revealed; and
- publishing of the wording of the court decision in the media.

189. The person infringing a protected trademark is held liable for the injury pursuant to the general rules on compensation of damages. The court may, when the circumstances of particular case allow, adjudge to the injured party the lump sum compensation which cannot be lower than the usual compensation which he would have received for particular use of subject matter of protection, if the use was lawful.

190. The court may order an interim measure at the request of the person who makes it credible that the trademark right or the right arising from the application has been infringed, or that such infringement is imminent. The interim measure may consist in the seizure or withdrawal from circulation of the articles used in infringement, or the measure of prohibiting continuation of any activities by way of which the infringement may be/is committed. Further to this type of interim measure, the court may also comply with the request of the person who makes it credible that the trademark right or the right arising from the application has been infringed, or that such infringement is imminent, or that irreparable harm is likely to occur, or that there is a reasonable suspicion that evidence will be destroyed or that it will not be possible to collect it later, to order an interim measure to secure evidence without giving prior notice to, or hearing the person from whom the evidence is to be collected. The securing of evidence is being realized through the inspection of premises, vehicles, books, documents, as well as the seizure of documents and infringing goods, questioning of witnesses and expert witnesses. Both types of measures may be requested even before filing a complaint, provided that subsequently a complaint is filed within thirty days from the date of rendering the decision on interim measure/on securing the evidence.

191. The Trademark Act prescribes that the provisions of the Civil Procedure Act[106] and the Enforcement Act[107] are to be applied as *lex generalis*. Also, damages-related claims should be resolved by application of provisions of the Contract and Torts Act.[108]

192. Further to civil law remedies, the Trademark Act lists certain types of conduct that are subject to (pseudo)criminal penalties. Namely, a legal person who has infringed a trademark right or a right arising from the registration application is sanctioned on grounds of corporate offence (in Serbian, *privredni prestup*) by a fine. A responsible person in a legal entity who is found to infringe a trademark right may also be fined. The infringing objects and the objects used for the perpetration of the corporate offence may be forfeited and the infringing objects may be destroyed. An entrepreneur who has infringed a trademark right or a right arising from the registration application is sanctioned on grounds of misdemeanour by a fine. The infringing objects in a misdemeanour and the objects used for perpetration of the misdemeanour may be forfeited and the infringing objects may be destroyed. Finally, a natural or legal person who acts as representative in the exercising of the rights under the Trademark Act without a power of attorney is sanctioned on grounds of misdemeanour by a fine. The responsible person in a legal entity may also be fined.

§10. Overlapping and Relation to Other Intellectual Property Rights

193. The Trademark Act lays down several rules with respect to the relation of trademark right with other intellectual property rights. First, when defining a sign which may be registered as a trademark, the Trademark Act prescribes that a sign which, by its appearance or content, infringes copyright and industrial property rights cannot be registered. Second, once registered, a trademark may not be used in a way to prohibit others from utilizing their name or address in accordance with good business practices. Third, the holder of a trademark cannot prohibit others from using the same or similar sign for marking their goods/services of a different type, except in the case of a well-known trademark. However, the holder of a registered famous trademark may prevent all third parties not having his consent from using the same or similar sign for marking goods/services which are not similar to those for which the trademark has been registered, if such use takes unfair advantage of, or is detrimental to, the distinctive character or the repute of the trademark.

194. There may be an overlapping between trademark right and other intellectual property rights, such as the registered indication of geographical origin or registered design. Indeed, the overlapping of design and trademark protection is clearly

106. Official Journal of the Republic of Serbia, n° 72/2011, 49/2013, 74/2013, 55/2014, 87/2018 and 18/2020.

107. *Ibid.*, n° 06/2015, 106/2016, 113/2017 and 54/2019.

108. Official Journal of the SFR Yugoslavia, n° 29/78, 39/85, 45/89; Official Journal of the FR Yugoslavia, n° 31/93; Official Journal of the Union of Serbia and Montenegro, n° 1/2003; Official Journal of the Republic of Serbia, n° 18/2020.

possible, given the fact that a sign protected by a trademark right may consist in colours or three-dimensional shapes. There is an evident interest of design right owners to register their 3D design as a 3D trademark, given the fact that a trademark protection may last as long as protection requirements are met and the fees are paid. The coexistence of a registered trademark and a registered indication of geographical origin may also occur. The Trademark Act lays down a specific rule with regard to the overlapping of collective/certification trademark and a registered indication of geographical origin. Namely, if the object of protection of a collective/certification trademark is a sign that implies a specific geographical area where the goods/services originated from, the user of a collective/certification trademark cannot prohibit others from using such a sign in accordance with good business practices or prohibit its use to users of identical or similar registered indication of geographical origin for the same or similar types of goods/services.

Chapter 5. Trade Names

§1. Sources – Legislation

195. In Serbian law, trade names are protected by the Act on Trade and Commerce[109] and by the Companies Act.[110] The Act on Trade and Commerce is the main source of unfair competition rules in Serbia. In addition, trade name protection is governed by the multilateral industrial property agreements ratified by Serbia, in particular the Paris Convention.

§2. Protection of Trade Names

196. The Act on Trade and Commerce, in particular its Articles 32 and 41, is the main source of law on trade names in Serbia. The Act prescribes a duty of a merchant to display its trade name in a visible manner. Along with its trade name, a merchant is obliged to display the basic information on the sales facility, as well as on the type of trading format, in accordance with the prescribed classification.

197. Any unauthorized use of another merchant's name may constitute an act of unfair competition. The Act on Trade and Commerce enumerates different types of behaviour that may represent an act of unfair competition, one of them being the trade in goods with name, data and shape which may reasonably generate confusion among the consumers as to the source, quality or other characteristics of such goods. For an act of unfair competition to be committed, it is irrelevant whether such name is registered as a trademark or a business (company) name. It is sufficient that a merchant had used another merchant's name contrary to the good business practices, i.e., in a manner capable of creating confusion among the consumers as to the source, quality and other characteristics of the goods. The confusion may take two forms. The direct confusion, also referred to as a product confusion, or confusion in a narrow sense, exists if the public confuses the goods/services in question, to which the sign is affixed or which are offered/rendered under the sign, with those of the 'original' merchant. The public believes that the goods/services offered under the sign originate from or are rendered by the merchant or with his consent. The indirect confusion, also known as origin confusion, or confusion in a broad sense, exists in case the public can distinguish the products/services from one another but, due to the degree of similarity of the signs and the similarity of goods/services in question, may believe that the products/services originate from merchants that are somehow economically linked.

198. The complaint on the grounds of unfair competition may be filed by a merchant (competitor) that suffered material damage or moral damage in the form of tarnishing of its business reputation. The complaint may be filed within six months

109. Official Journal of the Republic of Serbia, nº 52/2019.
110. *Ibid.*, nº 36/2011, 99/2011, 83/2014, 5/2015, 44/2018, 95/2018 and 91/2019.

following the day the plaintiff has become aware of the act of unfair competition, but not later than within three years following the day when the act terminated. The plaintiff may request:

– that an act of unfair competition be determined;
– that an act of unfair competition ceases;
– that material and moral damages are compensated.

199. The court may order a monetary compensation in particular if that is justified by the importance, duration or intensity of the act of unfair competition, the effect of such act on the activity of the plaintiff, or the purpose of the compensation. The court may order the publishing of the wording of its decision in the Official Journal of the RS. The court proceedings on grounds of unfair competition are expedited.

200. Trade names may also be protected as business (company) names under the Companies Act (Articles 22–30). A registered name, under which a company operates in the market, consists of a company name and other elements prescribed by the law. A company name is used to distinguish a company from other market participants. A company name may or may not be identical to a trademark owned by such company. The other elements of a registered name include the indication of a legal form (e.g., 'joint stock company' or 'limited liability company') and of the location of the company's registered office. The company's registered name may also include a designation of the scope of its activities. In its operations, a company may, in addition to its registered name, use also an abbreviated registered name. As a rule, a company's registered name has to be in the Serbian language, written either in the Cyrillic or in the Latin alphabet. However, a company's name may be in a foreign language or may comprise certain foreign words of characters written in the English version of the Latin alphabet, as well as Arabic or Roman numbers. A company may use with its registered name the coat of arms, flag, emblem, sign or other symbol of the RS or a foreign country, a Serbian territorial unit or autonomous province or an international organization, with the consent of competent body of that country, Serbian territorial unit or autonomous province, or international organization.

201. The Companies Act prescribes several rules on the choice of a name that may serve as a company name. First, a company's registered name may not be offensive to public morality, misleading with regard to the company's legal form, or misleading with regard to the company's predominant business activity. A registered name that is not compliant with the requirements cannot be registered with the register of economic operators. In case of a violation of this rule, the public attorney may bring legal action before the competent court against the company responsible for such violation to obtain a judgment ordering a change of name of the offending company. If an offending company fails to change its name within thirty days of the date when the judgment becomes final and enforceable, the register of economic operators shall ex officio initiate the procedure of enforced liquidation of the offending company. Second, a company name may not be identical to the name of another company. A company name must be different from the name of other legal entities so as not to be misleading with regard to the identity of another company. In case of a violation of these rules, an interested party may bring legal action before the competent court against the company responsible for such violation to obtain a judgment ordering a change of name of the offending company and/or an indemnification for any damage incurred. The legal action may be initiated within three years of the date of registration of the name of the offending company in accordance with the law on registration. A final and enforceable judgment ordering a change of name of an offending company shall be submitted by the court to the register of economic operators for the purpose of registration. If an offending company fails to change its name within thirty days of the date when the judgment becomes final and enforceable, the register of economic operators shall ex officio initiate the procedure of enforced liquidation of the offending company. Third, a company's registered name may include the name of the RS or its territorial unit or autonomous province, subject to prior consent from a competent authority, in accordance with the law. Also, a company's registered name may include the name of a foreign country or international organization, subject to consent from such country or international organization. Fourth, a company's registered name may contain the name of a natural person with the consent of such natural person or, if the natural person is deceased, with the consent of his/her legal heirs. If a member of a company is a natural person whose name is contained in the name of that company and if such natural person is no longer a member of the company, the name of that natural person may remain included in the company's name only with the consent of such natural person or, if the natural person is deceased, with the consent of his/her legal heirs.

202. A company's name cannot be transferred to another company, except as a result of a status change in which the name is acquired by the acquiring company from the transferor company, which is dissolved after such status change.

Chapter 6. Industrial Designs

§1. Sources – Legislation

203. Under Serbian law, a design may be protected by copyright law or by rules specifically applicable to industrial designs. Copyright law protection is examined in Chapter 1, while the protection of designs by industrial property rules will be examined in the present Chapter. The protection of industrial designs in Serbia is primarily regulated by the 2009 Act on the legal protection of industrial designs (hereinafter, the Industrial Design Act).[111] The Industrial Design Act was subsequently amended in 2015 and 2018.[112] With respect to the registration procedure, the Government of Serbia adopted the Regulation on the contents of the registry of applications and the registry of industrial designs, the mandatory elements of applications for a design registration, and the data published in the Official Journal of the IP Office (hereinafter, the Regulation).[113]

204. Both the Industrial Designs Act and the Regulation are generally harmonized with main sources of international intellectual property law, including the TRIPS Agreement, and the sources of EU law. The SFR of Yugoslavia, which Serbia was a part of, became party to the Hague Agreement concerning the international deposit of industrial designs (1925) on 28 November 1960. The Hague Act (1960) and Articles 1–7 of the Complementary Act of Stockholm (1967) were ratified on 25 November 1993 by the Federal Republic of Yugoslavia, which Serbia was a part of. Following the dissolution of the Union of Serbia and Montenegro, Serbia submitted to WIPO a Declaration of continuation on 19 September 2006.[114] Serbia also became party to the Geneva Act (1999) on 9 December 2009.[115] Further to joining the Hague Agreement, the SFR of Yugoslavia, which Serbia was a part of, acceded to the Locarno Agreement establishing an international classification for industrial designs (1968) on 8 October 1968.[116] Following the dissolution of SFR Yugoslavia, the Federal Republic of Yugoslavia, formed by Serbia and Montenegro, renewed the membership on 27 April 1992. In 2006, following the dissolution of the Union of Serbia and Montenegro, Serbia submitted to WIPO the abovementioned Declaration of continuation.

205. Also, the IP Office adopted its Methodological guidebook on industrial designs registration and other proceedings before the Office, which is available on its website.[117]

111. Official Journal of the Republic of Serbia, n° 104/2009.
112. *Ibid.*, n° 45/2015 and 44/2018.
113. *Ibid.*, n° 43/2010.
114. Official Journal of the Federal Republic of Yugoslavia – International Agreements, n° 3/1993.
115. *Ibid.*, n° 42/2009.
116. *Ibid.*, n° 51/1974.
117. The Methodological guidebook is available at: *http://www.zis.gov.rs* .

§2. Subject Matter of Protection

206. Under Article 2 of the Industrial Design Act, the notion of industrial design encompasses two-dimensional or three-dimensional appearance of the entire product or a part thereof, defined by its visual characteristics, in particular the lines, contours, colours, shape, texture and/or materials, or the combination thereof, of the product itself and/or its ornamentation. 'Product' means any industrial or handicraft item, including *inter alia* parts intended to be assembled into a complex product, packaging, get-up, graphic symbols and typographic typefaces, but excluding computer programs. A 'complex product' is a product which is composed of multiple components which can be replaced permitting disassembly and re-assembly of the product.

207. From this basic provision, it may be inferred that the industrial design protection is limited to the ornamental aspects of certain products. These aspects must be exterior and visible.[118] Furthermore, industrial design protection does not extend to the features of appearance of a product which are solely dictated by its technical function, nor to those which must necessarily be reproduced in their exact form and dimensions in order to permit the product in which the design is incorporated or to which it is applied to be mechanically connected to or placed in, around or against another product so that either product may perform its function. However, industrial design protection shall subsist in a design serving the purpose of allowing the multiple assembly or connection of mutually interchangeable products within a modular system.[119]

§3. Conditions of Protection

208. In order to be protected, an industrial design must meet both positive and negative requirements. Under the Industrial Design Act, a design must be new and have an individual character. Furthermore, a design must not be contrary to public order or morality, must not infringe intellectual property rights of other persons, must not contain state or any other public coat of arms, flag or emblem, name or abbreviated name of a country or an international organization, religious or national symbols, as well as imitations thereof, except under the consent by the competent authority, nor it could contain a well-known sign.[120]

118. *See* S. Marković, D. Popović, *supra,* 184–185.
119. *See* Industrial Design Act, Art. 8, paras. 1–3.
120. *Ibid.*, Arts 4–5, 8–9.

I. Individual Character

209. A design shall be considered to have individual character if the overall impression it produces on an informed user differs from the overall impression produced on such a user by any other design which has been made available to the public before the date of filling the application for registration or, if priority is claimed, the date of priority. In assessing individual character, the degree of freedom of a designer in developing the design shall be taken into consideration. An informed user, within the meaning of the Industrial Designs Act, is a natural person who is regularly in contact with the product concerned. Clearly, the legal standard of an 'informed user' is much higher than that of an 'average consumer' within the meaning of the Trademark Act.

210. Although the requirement of individual character of a design originates from the originality criterion laid down by copyright rules, the two concepts are not identical. In copyright law, originality stems from individual traits of each person, therefore authors working independently one from another cannot create identical works. The novelty criterion is not prescribed by copyright rules which allows for a finding of originality even in the absence of novelty. Under industrial property law, to the contrary, the individual character criterion has to coexist with that of novelty, which leads to its somewhat different interpretation. The individuality criterion is prescribed to prevent the transposing of a certain design from one type of product to another. For example, a design which is already applied to a kitchen bowl cannot be transposed onto a lamp, since it would not be considered having an individual character. An informed user would realize that such a design is already familiar to him/her, i.e., such a design would not produce a different overall impression.

II. Novelty

211. A design shall be considered to be new if no identical design has been made available to the public before the date of filling of the application for registration of the design for which the protection is claimed, or, if priority is claimed, the date of priority, or if there is no earlier application for registration of an identical design which became available to the public. Consequently, the novelty criterion is to be interpreted as an absolute novelty, as it is the case in patent law. Designs shall be deemed to be identical if their features differ only in immaterial details.

212. A design shall be deemed to have been made available to the public if it has been published following registration or otherwise, or exhibited, used in trade or otherwise disclosed before the date of filling of the application for registration of the design for which the protection is claimed, or, if priority is claimed, the date of priority, except where these events could not reasonably have become known in the normal course of business to the circles specialized in the sector concerned, operating within Serbia. However, the design shall not be deemed to have been made available to the public for the sole reason that it has been disclosed to a third person under explicit or implicit conditions of confidentiality. A design shall not be deemed disclosed if it has been made available to the public by the designer, his successor in title, or a third person as a result of information provided or action taken by the designer or his successor in title, during the twelve-month period preceding the date of filing of the application or, if a priority is claimed, the date of priority. Also, a design shall not be deemed disclosed if it has been made available to the public as a consequence of an abuse in relation to the designer or his successor in title.

III. Respect of Public Order and Morality

213. For a design to be legally protected, its publicizing or use must not be contrary to public order or to accepted principles of morality. The morality criterion is being assessed within the context of Serbian society; therefore, a design found to be in line with the principles of morality in a foreign country may still be found not to meet the same requirement in Serbia, and vice versa.

IV. Respect of Existing Intellectual Property Rights

214. A design for which the protection is claimed must not infringe existing intellectual property rights of other persons. With respect to industrial property rights, the fulfilment of this condition is being easily verified in the electronic database of applications and/or registered rights. However, the fulfilment of this requirement cannot be verified in the same manner with respect to copyright, due to non-formality of copyright protection. Therefore, the examiner of the application for a design protection could only determine whether the submitted design is identical or similar to a well-known copyrighted work. The authors of less known works could still initiate annulment proceedings if they find the registered design infringes their copyright.

215. The respect of existing intellectual property rights is not an absolute requirement. The owners of such rights could authorize the use of their protected intellectual goods as an element of other person's design.

V. Respect of State, Public and International Names and Symbols

216. A design for which the protection is claimed must not contain state or any other public coat of arms, flag or emblem, name or abbreviated name of a country or an international organization, religious or national symbols, as well as imitations thereof. However, this is not an absolute requirement. The state authorities and the competent organs of international organizations could authorize the use of such names and symbols as elements of a design for which the protection is claimed.

VI. Respect of Well-Known Signs

217. A design for which the protection is claimed must not contain a well-known sign, if the rules regulating the use of such a sign empower the right holder to prevent it. This rule should be interpreted as governing the use of notorious trade-marks, or names and images of historical or other well-known persons as elements of a design for which the protection is claimed. However this is not an absolute requirement. A right holder could always authorize the use of a well-known sign.

§4. Formalities: Procedure for Obtaining Protection

218. Protection of industrial designs is obtained by means of registration before the IP Office of the RS. The protection of unregistered designs is not prescribed under Serbian law. However, a design may be protected as a copyrighted work in case it fulfils the criteria laid down by the Copyright Act.

I. Application for an Industrial Design Registration

219. The procedure before the IP Office is initiated by filling an application for the industrial design right registration. The right to the industrial design protection is vested in the designer (also referred to as an 'author of a design' in Serbian legal doctrine), or his legal successor, or the employer in specific cases prescribed by the law.[121] Foreign natural and legal persons enjoy the national treatment if it results from international agreements or under reciprocity principle. A party invoking reciprocity between Serbia and a foreign country is supposed to submit the proof of its existence.[122] Foreign natural and legal persons must be represented by a local attorney or agent registered within the IP Office.

220. A written application for the industrial design right registration is to be submitted to the IP Office in person or by mail. Electronic application is not yet made possible. The mandatory elements of the application are:

– request for the protection of the industrial design;
– description of the industrial design; and
– two-dimensional depiction of the industrial design.

One application may contain the request for registration of one or multiple designs (up to hundred designs) applicable to products classified in the same class of the international classification set forth by the Locarno Agreement. The request for the registration of the industrial design must contain:

121. The provisions of the Patent Act governing the protection of inventions created by an employee apply *mutatis mutandis* to designs created in the employment context. *See* Industrial Design Act, Art. 47; Patent Act, Arts 57–66.
122. *See* Industrial Design Act, Art. 8a.

- applicant's personal data;
- designer's personal data, if that person is different from the applicant;
- if applicable, a statement by the designer indicating he/she waived the right to be cited in the application;
- in case the designer is not the applicant, a justification for filling of the application;
- indication on the quantity of designs for which the application is submitted;
- actual name and abbreviated name of a design; and
- signature of the applicant.

If the applicant wishes to defer the publication of a decision on registration for twelve months following its issuance, it should submit a request for non-disclosure along with the request for registration. A part from the explicit request for the registration of the industrial design, the application must contain a description of the industrial design. A description should be concise but detailed written presentation of the appearance of a design. It should not include information regarding the structure, function or functional advantages of the design or product onto which the design is materialized. The final part of the application for the industrial design right registration is the two-dimensional depiction of the industrial design. The depiction should provide clearly visible details of the design and should meet the prescribed requirements with respect to quality and other technical conditions.[123]

221. Once the application for the industrial design right registration is submitted and the procedural fees are paid, the IP Office examines the fulfilment of the above-mentioned formal requirements prescribed by the law. From the date of filling the application, the applicant shall enjoy a priority right. An international right of priority is recognized to natural and legal persons who filed an industrial design right application in any Member State of the Paris Union or the WTO within the time-frame of six months preceding the filing of application in Serbia. An exhibition priority right is recognized to applicants who exhibited the design at a national fair or international exhibition or in any other state of the Paris Union or the WTO within three months preceding the date of filing of the application before the Serbian IP Office.

II. Grant of an Industrial Design Right

222. If the formal requirements that an application for an industrial design right must satisfy have been met, the IP Office shall proceed to examining the fulfilment of substantive requirements. During this phase of the proceedings, an application for industrial design registration may be altered to become the application for patent or petty patent registration.[124] This alteration may occur only upon applicant's initiative.

---

123. The IP Office published on its website the Instructions for filling of national industrial design application.
124. *See* Industrial Design Act, Art. 35.

223. Where the application was found to meet the registration requirements – novelty, individual character and others – the IP Office shall issue a decision requesting the applicant to pay the registration fee for the first five years of registration, as well as the costs of industrial design publication, and submit the proof of payments made. Following this step, the IP Office shall issue the decision on the registration of the industrial design right, which will subsequently be entered into the Industrial Design Registry. The holder of the industrial design right shall be issued an industrial design certificate. The grant of an industrial design is published in the Official Journal of the IP Office.

224. However, if the IP Office establishes that the application does not meet the registration requirements, it shall notify the applicant in writing of the reasons due to which design cannot be granted and invite the applicant to submit its observations. Where the applicant fails to respond, or where the applicant responds but the IP Office nevertheless considers that the industrial design may not be registered, a decision on refusal of industrial design registration shall be issued. In case a multiple application has been submitted (for 2–100 industrial designs), the IP Office may decide to partially refuse the application.

§5. Ownership and Transfer: Assignment – Licenses

225. Ownership of the rights granted with regard to industrial designs belongs to the author of the latter. There is a rebuttable presumption to the effect that the first applicant for an industrial design registration is the author of such industrial design. If an industrial design is registered in favour of a person who is not the author, hair, legatee or assignee of the author, the rightful owners of the industrial design may file a special action to obtain registration and title with such industrial design.[125] Ownership of the rights with regard to industrial designs created in the employment context (e.g., under instructions received from an employer) is regulated by analogy to ownership of patents on inventions created by an employee.[126] If an industrial design has been jointly created by two or more persons, in a context other than an employment relationship, such persons shall have joint ownership of the rights granted with regard to an industrial design.

226. The rights granted with regard to industrial designs may be assigned. Assignment of industrial design rights and/or rights arising from the industrial design right application may result from the assignment agreement, change of status of the holder of the industrial design right and/or the applicant, or a court or administrative decision. Assignment is to be recorded in the appropriate registry of the IP Office. Registration of the assignment produces effects with respect to third parties. In case the assignment results from an assignment agreement, such an

125. *See* Industrial Design Act, Arts 71 and 74.
126. *See supra* Ch. 2, §5.

agreement should be concluded in written form and contain a designation of contracting parties, the indication of the quantity of registered industrial designs (or the application numbers), and the amount of remuneration, if stipulated.[127]

227. The holder of the industrial design right and/or the applicant may grant licence with respect to the right to use the registered industrial design and/or design for which the registration application is submitted, by entering into a licensing agreement. The agreement has to be concluded in writing and contain indication of the contracting parties, industrial design registration number or registration application number, the term of validity of the licence and the scope of the licence. The licence agreement is to be recorded in the appropriate registry of the IP Office. Registration of the licence agreement produces effects with respect to third parties.[128]

228. The rights granted with regard to industrial designs may be pledged. The holder of the industrial design right and/or the applicant may pledge the industrial design right and/or right arising from the industrial design registration application, by entering into an agreement of pledge. The agreement has to be concluded in written form and is to be recorded in the appropriate registry of the IP Office.[129]

§6. Scope of Exclusive Rights

229. A registered industrial design confers to its holder the exclusive right to use it and to prevent any third party not having his consent from using it. The aforementioned use covers, in particular, the making, offering, putting on the market, importing, exporting or using a product in which the design is incorporated or to which it is applied, or stocking such a product for those purposes. The author of industrial design has moral and economic rights. The only moral right a designer enjoys is the right to be recognized as the author of a design. This should be understood as the designer's right to have his name indicated in the registration application, documents and certificate of the industrial design. Further to this moral right, the author of an industrial design has the right to enjoy economic benefits from the use of the protected industrial design. Where the designer is not the holder of the industrial design right, the manner in which the designer shall enjoy economic benefits from the use of the protected industrial design shall be regulated by the contract concluded between the two.[130] The scope of exclusive economic rights is to be determined by analogy with the economic rights conferred by a patented invention or a protected trademark. The exclusive rights of the owner of an industrial design

127. *See* Industrial Design Act, Arts 49–50. General rules on contractual transfer of rights laid down by the Contract and Torts Act are also applicable.
128. *See* Industrial Design Act, Art. 51. General rules on license agreements laid down by the Contract and Torts Act are also applicable.
129. *See* Industrial Design Act, Art. 52. General rules on pledge of movable assets and rights are also applicable.
130. *See* Industrial Design Act, Arts 39–40.

extend not only to identical reproductions of the protected design, but also to non-identical imitations. Minor variations are not sufficient to prevent the finding of an infringement of the owner's exclusive rights.

§7. Exceptions and Limitations to Industrial Design Protection

230. The Industrial Design Act prescribes several limitations to exclusive protection of a registered design. The rights conferred by a registered industrial design cannot be exercised in respect of acts done privately and for non-commercial purposes, acts done for experimental purposes, and acts of reproduction for the purpose of making citations or of teaching, provided that such acts are compatible with fair trade practice and do not unduly prejudice the normal exploitation of the design, and that mention is made of the source. Further to this, the rights conferred by a registered industrial design cannot be exercised in respect of the equipment on ships and aircraft registered in a third country when these temporarily enter the territory of the RS, the importation in the RS of spare parts and accessories for the purpose of repairing such craft, and the execution of repairs on such craft.[131]

231. The classical doctrine of exhaustion of intellectual property rights applies to industrial design rights as well. The rights conferred by a registered industrial design shall not extend to acts relating to a product in which a design included within the scope of protection of the registered design is incorporated or to which it is applied, when the product has been put on the market in the RS by the holder of the industrial design right or with his consent.[132]

232. Finally, in case a third person who can establish that before the date of the filing of the application or, if priority is claimed, before the date of priority, has in good faith commenced use within the territory of the RS, or has made serious and effective preparations to that end, of a design included within the scope of protection of an industrial design right, and which has not been copied from the latter, the holder of the industrial design right has to tolerate that such a person exploits the design for the purposes for which its use had been effected, or for which serious and effective preparations had been made, before the filing or priority date. This right of prior use has an *inter partes* effect, therefore cannot extend to granting a licence to another person to exploit the design. The right of prior use can only be transferred exceptionally, where the third person is a business, along with that part of the business in the course of which the act was done or the preparations were made.[133]

131. *Ibid.*, Arts 43–44.
132. *Ibid.*, Art. 45. *See also* Dušan Popović, *Isključiva prava intelektualne svojine i slobodna konkurencija*, Pravni fakultet Univerziteta u Beogradu, Belgrade, 2012, 173–191.
133. *See* Industrial Design Act, Art. 42.

§8. Duration of Protection

233. A design which meets the requirements prescribed by the Industrial Design Act is protected, upon registration by the IP Office, for a period of five years as of from the date of the filing of the application. The right holder may have the term of protection renewed for one or more periods of five years each, up to a total term of twenty-five years from the date of filing. Registration of the registered design may be renewed at the request of the right holder or of any person expressly authorized by him, provided that the renewal fee has been paid. The contents of such request are prescribed by the Regulation on the contents of the registry of applications and the registry of industrial designs, the mandatory elements of applications for a design registration, and the data published in the Official Journal of the IP Office.[134] The industrial design right may cease not only in case the right holder fails to pay the prescribed fee for maintenance of the right, but also:

- if the right holder abandons the right, on the day following the day of filing the statement of abandonment;
- based on a court decision, or a decision of an administrative authority, on the day designated in such decision, due to lack of substantive conditions required for industrial design protection, particularly if the registered holder is not the author of the design or an assignee, heir or legatee of such author;
- if the legal person has been dissolved, or if the natural person who is the right holder has deceased, on the day of dissolution of the legal person, or death of natural person, unless the design right has been transferred to legal successors of such persons.[135]

§9. Infringement and Remedies

234. The infringement of the exclusive rights of the owner of an industrial design results in civil and criminal remedies. For these remedies to apply, the industrial design has to be duly registered in proceedings before the IP Office. If a design is not registered but is used in the course of trade, the applicable remedies are those on unfair competition.[136]

235. Civil law remedies are primarily regulated by the Industrial Design Act.[137] Similarly to rules applicable in other jurisdiction, in Serbia an industrial design right infringement consists in any unauthorized exploitation of a registered design or the unauthorized publication of a design for which the protection is claimed. Imitation of a protected industrial design is also considered to be an infringement. The complaint on the grounds of infringement of a design right may be filed by the applicant, holder of the industrial design right and the acquirer of exclusive licence. The

134. *See* Regulation, Art. 28.
135. *See* Industrial Design Act, Arts 11, 56.
136. In particular, the rules on protection against slavish imitation.
137. *See* Industrial Design Act, Arts 63–74a.

latter may file a complaint if the exclusive licence agreement does not stipulate the contrary. The complaint for infringement of the industrial design right may be filed within three years following the day the plaintiff has become aware of the infringement and the infringer, but not later than within five years following the day when infringement was committed for the first time. In case of infringement of the industrial design right, the plaintiff may request, *inter alia*:

- that infringement of the right be determined;
- cessation of the infringement of right;
- that the articles used in infringement of the right be destroyed or modified;
- that the tools and equipment used for production of the articles used in infringement of the right be destroyed or modified, if that is necessary for the efficient protection of the right;
- compensation for material damages and reasonable costs of procedure;
- compensation for moral damages;
- information on any third persons participating in infringement of the right to be revealed; and
- publishing of the wording of the court decision in the media.

The person infringing the industrial design right is held liable for the injury pursuant to the general rules on compensation of damages. The court may, when the circumstances of particular case allow, adjudge to the injured party the lump sum compensation which cannot be lower than the usual compensation which he would have received for particular use of subject matter of protection, if the use was lawful.

236. The court may order an interim measure at the request of the person who makes it credible that the industrial design right or the right arising from the application has been infringed, or that such infringement is imminent. The interim measure may consist in the seizure or withdrawal from circulation of the articles used in infringement, or the measure of prohibiting continuation of any activities by way of which the infringement may be/is committed. Further to this type of interim measure, the court may also comply with the request of the person who makes it credible that the industrial design right or the right arising from the application has been infringed, or that such infringement is imminent, or that irreparable harm is likely to occur, or that there is a reasonable suspicion that evidence will be destroyed or that it will not be possible to collect it later, to order an interim measure to secure evidence without giving prior notice to, or hearing the person from whom the evidence is to be collected. The securing of evidence is being realized through the inspection of premises, vehicles, books, documents, as well as the seizure of documents and infringing goods, questioning of witnesses and expert witnesses. Both types of measures may be requested even before filing a complaint, provided that subsequently a complaint is filed within thirty days from the date of rendering the decision on interim measure/on securing the evidence.

237. The Industrial Design Act prescribes that the provisions of the Civil Procedure Act[138] and the Enforcement Act[139] are to be applied as *lex generalis*. Also, damages-related claims should be resolved by subsidiary application of provisions of the Contract and Torts Act.[140]

238. Further to civil law remedies, the Industrial Design Act lists certain types of conduct that are subject to (pseudo) criminal penalties. Namely, a legal person who has infringed an industrial design right or a right arising from the registration application is sanctioned on grounds of corporate offence (in Serbian, *privredni prestup*) by a fine. A responsible person in a legal entity who is found to infringe industrial design right may also be fined. The infringing objects and the objects used for the perpetration of the corporate offence may be forfeited and the infringing objects may be destroyed. An entrepreneur who has infringed an industrial design right or a right arising from the registration application is sanctioned on grounds of misdemeanour by a fine. The infringing objects in a misdemeanour and the objects used for perpetration of the misdemeanour may be forfeited and the infringing objects may be destroyed. Finally, a legal person who acts as representative in the exercising of the rights under the Industrial Designs Act without a power of attorney is sanctioned on grounds of misdemeanour by a fine. The responsible person in a legal entity may also be fined.[141]

239. The Penal Code prescribes criminal responsibility for acts of unauthorized use of a design protected by an industrial design right or a right arising from registration application. Such unauthorized use shall be sanctioned with a fine or imprisonment up to three years. An act of unauthorized publishing of a previously unpublished industrial design protected by the law shall be sanctioned with a fine or imprisonment up to one year. The infringing objects shall be seized.[142]

§10. Overlapping and Relation to Other Intellectual Property Rights

240. The Industrial Design Act lays down a single provision regarding the interaction of a subjective industrial design right with other intellectual property rights. Under Article 46 of the Act, the provisions providing specific protection of industrial designs shall not affect any existing rights with respect to trademarks and other distinctive signs, patents, petty patents or topographies of semiconducting products.

138. Official Journal of the Republic of Serbia, n° 72/2011, 49/2013, 74/2013, 55/2014, 87/2018 and 18/2020.
139. *Ibid.*, n° 06/2015, 106/2016, 113/2017 and 54/2019.
140. Official Journal of the SFR Yugoslavia, n° 29/78, 39/85, 45/89; Official Journal of the FR Yugoslavia, n° 31/93; Official Journal of the Union of Serbia and Montenegro, n° 1/2003; Official Journal of the Republic of Serbia, n° 18/2020.
141. *See* Industrial Design Act, Arts 75–77.
142. *See* Penal Code, Official Journal of the Republic of Serbia, n° 85/2005, 88/2005, 107/2005, 72/2009, 111/2009, 121/2009, 104/2013,108/2014, 94/2016 and 35/2019, Art. 202. For a detailed analysis of criminal offenses against intellectual property *see*: Z. Stojanović, N. Delić, *Krivično pravo-Posebni deo,* Pravni fakultet Univerziteta u Beogradu, Pravna knjiga, Belgrade 2013, 123–133.

The same is prescribed with respect to unregistered designs, and the application of rules on unfair competition and rules on civil law responsibility.

241. A design may be protected by copyright law if it meets the criteria prescribed by the Copyright Act – if it is original and expressed in a certain form, *inter alia.* The copyright protection is established as of the date of creation of a design (principle of non-formality of copyright protection). The owner of rights with regard to such designs under the Copyright Act and the Industrial Design Act may choose to exercise the rights and legal actions derived from one or the other intellectual property, in a given case, but may not simultaneously claim protection under both regimes.[143]

242. As already explained, an application for industrial design registration may be altered to become the application for patent or petty patent registration if it is concluded that the functional elements of the intellectual creation prevail over its ornamental characteristics. Also, an applicant for petty patent protection may request from the IP Office to alter its petty patent application into a patent or design right application, and vice versa.[144]

243. Finally, as examined *supra* in the context of the analysis of trademark right, the overlapping of design and trademark protection is clearly possible, given the fact that a sign protected by a trademark right may consist in colours or three-dimensional shapes.

143. *See* S. Marković, D. Popović, *supra,* 192.
144. *See* Patent Act, Art. 166.

Chapter 7. Plant Varieties

§1. Sources – Legislation

244. In Serbia, plant varieties are protected under the Plant Breeders' Rights Act.[145] Contrary to other forms of industrial property protection in Serbia, the protection of plant varieties is not the competence of the IP Office of the RS; it is the Ministry of Agriculture that is entrusted with the enforcement of this Act. The registration of plant varieties and the entering of their official denomination in the registry of the Ministry of Agriculture are regulated under the Act on the registration of agricultural plant varieties.[146] Plant variety protection also results from the ratification by the RS of the International Convention for the Protection of New Varieties of Plants (hereinafter, UPOV). Serbia became a member of UPOV on 5 January 2013.

245. Patent protection of plant varieties is excluded under Serbian law. Under the exceptions to patentability, the Patent Act indicates plant or animal varieties or essentially biological processes for the production of a plant or animal, except microbiological processes or the products obtained by means of such processes.[147]

§2. Subject Matter of Protection

246. The Plant Breeders' Rights Act grants protection to plant varieties. A plant variety is defined as a plant grouping within a single botanical taxon of the lowest known rank which, irrespective of whether the conditions for the grant of a breeder's right are fully met, can be:

- defined by the expression of the characteristic resulting from a given genotype or combination of genotypes;
- distinguished from any other plant grouping by the expression of at least one of the said characteristics; and
- considered as a unit with regard to its suitability for being propagated unchanged.[148]

When defining the scope of breeder's right, the legislator clarified that the protection is extended to varieties which are essentially derived from the protected variety, where the protected variety is not itself an essentially derived variety, to varieties that are not clearly distinguishable from the protected variety, and to varieties whose production requires the repeated use of the protected variety.[149]

145. Official Journal of the Republic of Serbia, n° 41/2009 and 88/2011.
146. *Ibid.*, n° 30/2010.
147. *See* Patent Act, Art. 9, para. 1.
148. *See* Plant Breeders' Protection Act, Art. 2.
149. *Ibid.*, Art. 25.

247. Although plant variety protection does not require inventive activity or a certain inventive level, as it is the case with respect to patentable inventions, such protection does require a minimum level of creativity or development attributable to the originator of a protected variety. This minimum development or discovery is referred to as a 'distinctiveness of a plant variety', which is prescribed as one of the conditions for legal protection of plant varieties in Serbian law.

§3. Conditions of Protection

248. Under the Plant Breeders' Rights Act, the following conditions are required for the protection of plant variety: novelty, distinctiveness, uniformity and stability.[150] A variety is considered new if, at the date of filing of the application for a breeder's right, propagating or harvested material of the variety has not been sold or otherwise disposed of to others, by or with the consent of the breeder, for purposes of exploitation of the variety in the RS earlier than one year, or within foreign territory earlier than four years, and in the case of vine and tree varieties earlier than six years before the filing date. The variety shall be deemed to be new if it is disposed to others:

- by a contract on the transfer of rights to the successor in title;
- by a contract on disposal of variety material between companies related through capital, where one company is owner of another company, or between companies that are owned by a third company, provided that the disposal is not for purpose of exploiting the variety;
- by an agreement under which a person multiplies propagating material of a variety on behalf of the breeder, where that agreement requires that the property in the multiplied material reverts to the breeder; and
- by a contract on testing in trial fields or laboratory for the purpose of variety evaluation.

A variety shall be deemed to be new if availability of such variety by the breeder is the result of presenting such variety in exhibitions officially recognized pursuant to the Convention on International Exhibitions, concluded on 22 November 1928 in Paris.

249. The condition of distinctiveness implies that a variety is clearly distinguishable from any other variety whose existence is a matter of common knowledge at the time of filing of the application for breeder's right protection. For example, the filing of an application for the granting of the breeder's right or for the entering of a variety in the official registry of varieties, in any country or intergovernmental organization, is considered to render the variety a matter of common knowledge, from the date of the application.

150. *Ibid.*, Arts 6–10.

250. The condition of uniformity implies that a variety is sufficiently homogeneous in its relevant characteristics. In the assessment of this criterion, variations that may be expected from the particular features of propagation of a variety are being tolerated. The fulfilment of this condition is being determined statistically by a competent authority, usually the agricultural institute acting on behalf of the Ministry of Agriculture. Under the condition of stability, it is required that the most relevant hereditary characteristics of a plant variety remained as defined after successive propagations, or in the case of a special propagation cycle, at the end of each of such cycles. Both the condition of homogeneity and the condition of stability must be identified throughout the process of examination before the competent authority.

§4. Formalities: Procedure for Obtaining Protection

251. Protection of plant varieties is obtained by means of registration before the Ministry of Agriculture of the RS. The registration procedure is regulated under the Plant Breeders' Rights Act and the General Administrative Procedure Act.

I. Application for Plant Breeder's Right Registration

252. The procedure for the grant of the plant breeder's right is initiated by filing an application for plant breeder's right registration before the Ministry of Agriculture.[151] The application may be filed by the breeder himself or his authorized representative. Further to the application, the applicant must submit the documents on the breeding history of the variety and the proposal of the variety denomination. Upon the request from the Ministry, the applicant has to provide appropriate samples of propagating material of the variety for testing. Samples, as well as documents related to such variety materials, are treated as confidential information. Upon the receipt of the application, the Ministry shall determine whether the application is complete within the meaning of the General Administrative Procedure Act and the Plant Breeders' Rights Act. If deficiencies are detected, the Ministry shall invite the applicant to remove them within the prescribed time limit.

253. A breeder is supposed to propose the variety denomination in the plant breeder's right application. The Ministry of Agriculture has the duty to inform competent authorities of all UPOV members on issues related to the denomination of a variety, particularly on the proposal, registration and cancellation of the denomination for a variety. Competent authorities of UPOV members may submit their objections regarding denominations to the Ministry. The variety is supposed to be designated by a denomination which represents its generic designation. The denomination:

– must enable the variety to be identified;

151. *Ibid.*, Arts 15–22.

- must not consist solely of numbers except where this is an established practice for designating varieties;
- must not be liable to mislead or to cause confusion concerning the characteristics, value or identity of the variety or the identity of the breeder; in particular, it has to be different from every denomination which designates, in the territory of any member of UPOV, an existing variety of the same plant species or of a closely related species; and
- cannot be unsuitable for usage in the RS.

Where the variety is already protected in the UPOV Member State or where an application for the protection of the same variety is filed in a member of UPOV, only the variety denomination which has been proposed or registered in that other Member State may be submitted within the RS by the breeder.

254. If the variety denomination does not meet the prescribed criteria, the Ministry of Agriculture shall cancel the denomination registration. The cancellation may also result from the court decision forbidding the use of a given denomination. If a variety denomination is cancelled, the Ministry shall notify the breeder thereof and invite him to submit a proposal of a new denomination.

255. Under the Plant Breeders' Rights Act, any person who offers for sale or markets the propagating material of a protected variety must use the registered variety denomination. A trademark, trade name or another similar identification may be used along with the registered variety denomination provided that denomination is easily recognizable. The obligation to use the registered variety denomination does not cease after the expiration of plant variety protection, except where prior rights of third persons prevent such use.

256. The application which is assessed as complete by the Ministry of Agriculture, including the proposed variety denomination, is consequently entered into the Registry of applications, kept by the Ministry and available on its website. The following data are recorded in the Registry of applications:

- name of a breeder or his authorized representative;
- permanent residence or seat of a breeder or his authorized representative;
- proposed denomination of a variety and plant species; and
- date and time of receipt of the application.

Access to data recorded in the Registry of applications is generally allowed, except with regard to data deemed confidential under the Plant Breeders' Rights Act.

257. In line with general rules of industrial property law, the right of priority is recognized with respect to the plant varieties' protection as well. Namely, a breeder who has duly filed an application for the grant of a breeder's right with the competent authority of another UPOV Member State, shall enjoy the right of priority within the RS for a period of twelve months from the date of his first application, the day of filing not being included in that period. In order to benefit from the right of priority, a breeder has to, in the subsequent application, claim the priority of the first application and within three months of filing the application for granting of the breeder's right to submit the relevant documents and samples to the Ministry of Agriculture. If the Ministry accepts the proof regarding the priority date, the application shall be deemed to have been filed on the day of filing of the first application.

258. The entry of an application into the Registry kept by the Ministry of Agriculture may be objected to on two different grounds.[152] First, a person who considers that the proposed variety denomination does not fulfil the conditions prescribed by the Plant Breeders' Rights Act may submit to the Ministry an objection to the proposal of the denomination entered into the Registry of applications. The Ministry shall then invite the breeder to respond to the objection and possibly propose a new variety denomination. If it finds that the proposed variety denomination does not meet the requirements prescribed by the law, the Ministry shall invite the breeder to propose a new denomination. In case a breeder ignores such an invitation, the Ministry shall reject the application for a breeder's right registration. Second, a person who considers that a variety which has been entered into the Registry of applications does not meet the criteria prescribed by the Plant Breeders' Rights Act, or that the applicant does not have a right to protection, may object to the Ministry of Agriculture's decision. A party filing such an objection must submit proof for its claims. The Ministry may also decide to undertake additional verifications.

II. Grant of a Plant Breeder's Right

259. If the formal requirements that an application for a plant breeder's right must satisfy have been met, the Ministry of Agriculture shall proceed to examining the fulfilment of substantive requirements. The Ministry shall normally delegate the activities related to variety examination to a legal entity that in terms of expertise and equipment is prepared to undertake such examinations. The Ministry could also decide to accept the results of previously conducted examinations of a variety. The Ministry may use results of technical examination of a variety obtained in another UPOV Member State or in a country with which Serbia is linked by a bilateral or another multilateral agreement. The decision on fulfilment of conditions is final and administrative dispute proceedings may be instituted against it before the Administrative Court of the RS.

260. The Ministry of Agriculture adopts its decision upon the proposal from the Expert Council containing a recommendation to grant a plant breeder's right or to reject the application.[153] Normally, a decision granting a plant breeder's right should be interpreted as approving the proposed variety denomination as well. However, the Expert Council may object to the proposed variety denomination. The variety

152. *Ibid.*, Arts 20–21.
153. *Ibid.*, Art. 22.

that has been granted protection is subsequently entered into the Registry of protected plant varieties, kept by the Ministry of Agriculture. This registry contains the same category of data as the Registry of applications, and is also freely available on the website of the Ministry.

§5. Ownership and Transfer: Assignment – Licenses

261. Ownership of the rights to a plant variety belongs to the person who bred or discovered and developed such variety. If two or more persons have mutually bred, or discovered and developed the variety, a joint ownership of the exclusive rights of the new variety would result. If two or more breeders have independently one from another bred, or discovered and developed the variety, the breeder's right shall be granted to the first breeder that filed the application for granting of a breeder's right. Foreign citizens enjoy the same rights as Serbian nationals, if such treatment is guaranteed by international treaties which the RS is a party of. Still, in proceedings before the Ministry of Agriculture, foreign citizens must be represented by persons having domicile in the RS. The ownership of a plant breeder's right may also reside within the employer of the person who bred, or discovered and developed a variety in the course of his/her employment, or within the employer that commissioned the breeding.[154]

262. The rights to plant varieties are assignable.[155] The owner of breeder's right may transfer its right, in part or entirely, to another person by means of a contract. The contract has to be concluded in writing. At the request of one of the parties, the contract is entered into the Registry of transferred breeders' rights, kept by the Ministry of Agriculture. The contract that is not recorded in the Registry of transferred breeders' rights will not have *erga omnes* effect. The name of the contractual parties, their addresses/seats, date and number of the contract, and the denomination of a plant variety, shall be recorded in the Registry.

263. The holder of the plant breeder's right may grant licence with respect to the right to use the registered plant variety, by entering into a licensing agreement.[156] The agreement has to be concluded in writing and contain indication of the contracting parties, plant variety registration number, the term of validity of the licence, the scope of the licence and the agreed compensation for such rights. The licence agreement is to be recorded in the appropriate registry of licenses. Registration of the licence agreement produces effects with respect to third parties.

154. *Ibid.*, Arts 4–5.
155. *Ibid.*, Art. 29.
156. *Ibid.*, Art. 30.

§6. Scope of Exclusive Rights

264. A breeder has a moral right to indicate his name in the application for granting of a breeder's right and in the accompanying documentation, as well as in the registries and other official records and documents kept by the competent public authorities. A registered plant variety confers to its holder the exclusive right to use its propagating material and to prevent any third party not having his consent from using it. The aforementioned use covers, in particular, the production or reproduction (multiplication), conditioning for the purpose of propagation, offering for sale, selling or other marketing, exporting and importing, and stocking for any of the abovementioned purposes.[157] These acts in respect of harvested material, including entire plants and parts of plants, obtained through the unauthorized use of the propagating material of the protected variety, also require the authorization of the holder of the breeder's right, unless the right holder has had reasonable opportunity to exercise his right in relation to the said propagating material. Furthermore, the mentioned acts in respect of products made directly from harvested material of the protected variety through the unauthorized use of the harvested material require the authorization of the right holder, unless the latter has had reasonable opportunity to exercise his right in relation to the said harvested material.

265. The exclusive rights also exist with respect to the use of varieties which are essentially derived from the protected variety, where the protected variety is not in itself an essentially derived variety, varieties which are not clearly distinguishable from the protected variety, and varieties whose production requires the repeated use of the protected variety. A variety is considered to be essentially derived from another variety when it is predominantly derived from the initial variety, or from a variety that is itself predominantly derived from the initial variety, while retaining the expression of the essential characteristics that result from the genotype or from the combination of genotypes of the initial variety. Also, in order to be considered an 'essentially derived', a variety has to be clearly distinguishable from the initial variety and has to conform to the initial variety in the expression of the essential characteristics that result from the genotype or combination of genotypes of the initial variety, except for the differences which result from the act of derivation itself.

§7. Exceptions and Limitations to Plant Variety Protection

266. The Plant Breeders' Rights Act prescribes several limitations to exclusive protection of a registered plant variety.[158] The rights conferred by a registered plant variety cannot be exercised in respect of acts done privately and for non-commercial purposes, acts done for experimental purposes, and acts done for the purpose of breeding other varieties, bearing in mind the explanations given with respect to the scope of the plant breeder's right. For a variety of plant species that is included in the list of species of agricultural plants involving exceptions to the

157. *Ibid.*, Art. 25.
158. *Ibid.*, Arts 26–27.

plant breeder's rights, it is considered that plant breeders' rights shall not be infringed by a farmer who, within reasonable limits and subject to the safeguarding of the legitimate interests of the breeders, uses for propagating purposes, on his own holding, the product of the harvest which he has obtained by planting, on his own holding, the protected variety, or the variety which is essentially derived from the protected variety where the protected variety is not in itself an essentially derived variety, or the variety which is not clearly distinguishable from the protected variety ('farm saved seed'). This list of species does not include the varieties of fruit, ornamentals, vegetables and forest trees. Agricultural producers, except for those classified as small agricultural producers, are obliged to pay to the right holder a reasonable remuneration for using of the farm saved seed. However, this remuneration has to be significantly lower than the one payable for the purchased seed. At the request of the breeder, agricultural producers must provide in writing all data the use of farm saved seed.

267. The doctrine of exhaustion of intellectual property rights applies to plant breeders' rights as well. The rights conferred by a registered plant variety shall not extend to acts concerning any material of the protected variety, or of a variety which is essentially derived from the protected variety, where the protected variety is not in itself an essentially derived variety, a variety which is not clearly distinguishable from the protected variety, and a variety whose production requires the repeated use of the protected variety, which has been sold or otherwise marketed by the breeder, or with his consent, in the RS, unless such acts involve further propagation of the variety in question, or exports of the materials of the variety, which enables the propagation of the variety, into a country which does not protect varieties of the plant genus or species to which the variety belongs, export where the exported material is for final consumption purposes. A material of the protected variety implies the propagating material of any kind, the harvested material including entire plants and parts of plants, and any product made directly from the harvested material.

268. Similarly to the legal regime of patented inventions, registered plant varieties may be subject to compulsory licenses as well. If a holder of a plant breeder's right refuses to enter into licensing agreement with the interested party, or sets unreasonable conditions for such a contract, the Ministry of Agriculture may, at the request of the interested party, grant a compulsory licence.[159] A compulsory licence may be granted only if this is necessary for the protection of the general interest, which should be interpreted as any national or other exceptional necessity for the protection of health and food of the population, protection of public interest in areas of vital significance to social, economic and technological development. The compulsory licence may be granted if a right holder does not exercise or insufficiently exercises its rights concerning the protected plant variety in the RS. The person interested in acquiring the licence must prove that it disposes of sufficient capacities for the use of the protected variety. The compulsory licence shall not be issued if the right holder proves that there are reasons justifying the non-exercise or insufficient exercise of the rights concerning the protected variety.

159. *Ibid.*, Arts 31–35.

269. The compulsory licence may not be granted as an exclusive one. Its scope and duration are limited to the reasons of public interest that justified its granting. A person who acquired a compulsory licence has to pay an equitable remuneration for the use of the protected variety. If the exact amount and modality of payment cannot be agreed on with the right holder, the remuneration shall be determined by the court. The breeder's right holder is obliged to deliver, as requested by the Ministry of Agriculture, the quantity of propagating material necessary for the exploitation of the compulsory licence, to the person to whom the compulsory licence has been granted. The latter is obliged to pay equitable remuneration to the right holder for such material. The amount and modality of payment is agreed between the parties. In the absence of such an agreement, the amount and modality of payment shall be determined by the competent court.

§8. Duration of Protection

270. A plant variety which meets the requirements prescribed by the Plant Breeders' Rights Act is protected, upon registration by the Ministry of Agriculture, for a period of twenty-five years from the date of the grant of the breeder's right, with the exception of varieties of potatoes, trees and vines which are protected for a period of thirty years from the date of the grant of the breeder's right.[160] This provision is in line with the UPOV Convention, which prescribes the minimum duration of protection of twenty years from the grant of the right.[161] The Serbian legislator harmonized the duration of protection of plant varieties with that prescribed under the European Union Regulation on Community Plant Variety Rights.[162]

271. Breeder's right may be terminated before the expiry of its prescribed duration period if the right holder submits to the Ministry of Agriculture a written statement indicating that it wishes to terminate the breeder's right. The termination shall produce effects on the date indicated in such a statement, or on the day of receipt of the statement. Also, a decision on the grant of a breeder's right may be cancelled if the right holder fails to pay the prescribed fee for maintenance of the right, if it is established that the protected variety is no longer uniform or stable, if the right holder fails to provide the Ministry with the information, documents or material deemed necessary for verifying the maintenance of the variety, or if the breeder fails to propose another denomination, in case the denomination is cancelled following the grant of the right.[163]

272. Finally, the Ministry of Agriculture may ex officio at the request of the interested party initiate proceedings aiming at declaring the nullity of a decision on

160. *Ibid.*, Art. 23.
161. *See* UPOV Convention, Art. 19.
162. *See* Regulation n° 2100/94 on Community Plant Variety Rights, Official Journal, n° L227 of 1.9.1994, Art. 19.
163. *Ibid.*, Arts 36, 38.

the grant of breeder's right. The nullity may be declared if, during the validity period of protection of the registered variety, it is determined that the variety was not new or distinct at the time of the grant of the breeder's right, or that the grant has been essentially based upon documents and information provided by the breeder and the variety was not uniform or stable at the time of the grant of the breeder's right, or that the right was granted to a person not entitled to it.[164]

§9. Infringement and Remedies

273. Infringements of the exclusive rights on plant varieties are subject to civil and criminal remedies. Both types of remedies are regulated under the Plant Breeders' Rights Act, with the subsidiary application of general rules on civil and criminal procedure, and rules on the assessment of damages.

274. Civil remedies consist of the indemnification of any damages caused by the infringement of a plant breeder's right.[165] A right owner whose right has been infringed may, in addition to compensation for damages, seek that the infringer be banned from further conduct of activities constituting such violation, as well as to have the judgment determining the infringement be published at the cost of the defendant. The infringement proceedings may be initiated within three years following the day the plaintiff has become aware of the infringement and the infringer, but not later than within five years following the day when infringement was committed.

275. Further to civil law responsibility for violation of a protected plant variety, the Plant Breeders' Rights Act lists certain types of conduct that are subject to (pseudo) criminal penalties.[166] Namely, a corporation or any other legal person who violates a protected variety is sanctioned on grounds of corporate offence (in Serbian, *privredni prestup*) by a fine. The violation may consist in unauthorized use of a denomination of a protected variety for any other existing variety belonging to the same plant species or closely related species, or unauthorized offering for sale or other marketing of propagating material of a protected variety, without using the registered variety denomination. A responsible person in a legal entity or a natural person acting independently who is found to infringe a plant breeder's right may also be fined. In addition to fines, the court may impose a protective measure consisting in prohibiting the infringer to perform a business activity for a certain period of time, or in case of a natural person – a prohibition to conduct certain duties. Finally, any natural or legal person who fails to deliver the propagating material at the request of the competent authority, as prescribed under the Plant Breeders' Rights Act, shall be sanctioned on grounds of misdemeanour by a fine.

---

164. *Ibid.*, Art. 37.
165. *Ibid.*, Arts 40–41.
166. *Ibid.*, Arts 48–50.

§10. Overlapping and Relation to Other Intellectual Property Rights

276. Patent protection of plant varieties is excluded under Serbian law, so no overlapping between patent and plant variety protection is possible.[167] A variety denomination may be protected as a trademark. Since there are no special rules, a variety denomination could enjoy trademark protection only if it meets the general requirements prescribed under the Trademark Act, in particular the distinctiveness requirement.[168]

167. *See* Patent Act, Art. 9, para. 1.
168. *See* Trademark Act, Arts 4–6.

Chapter 8. Topographies of Semiconducting Products

§1. Sources – Legislation

277. Under Serbian law, topographies of semiconducting products are protected by specific rules enacted by the Act on the legal protection of semiconducting products (hereinafter, Topographies of Semiconducting Products Act).[169] With respect to the registration procedure, the Government adopted the Regulation on the procedure of protecting the topographies of integrated circuits.[170] The Socialist Federal Republic of Yugoslavia, which Serbia was a part of, signed the International Treaty on Intellectual Property in Respect of Integrated Circuits – the Washington Treaty (1989)[171] on 26 May 1989. This Treaty has not yet entered into force. However, members of the WTO have to comply with the main provisions of the Washington Treaty. WTO members are bound to accord the treatment provided for in the TRIPS Agreement to the natural and legal persons who meet the criteria of eligibility for protection provided for under the Washington Treaty. This obligation applies irrespective of the fact that the Washington Treaty remained 'dead letter'. Even though Serbia has not yet acceded to the WTO, it already fulfilled this requirement by joining the Washington Treaty and subsequently adopting the national rules on the protection of layout designs of integrated circuits.

278. Although the protection of layout designs was made possible in Serbia for decades, there is not yet a single application for registration of topography of semiconducting products.[172] This could be explained by the fact that Serbia is not a significant producer of products which represent a materialization of topographies of semiconducting products.

§2. Subject Matter of Protection

279. As defined by the Topographies of Semiconducting Products, the notion of semiconducting product encompasses all final or intermediate forms of any product consisting of a body of material which includes a layer of semiconducting material and having one or more other layers composed of conducting, insulating or semiconducting material, the layers being arranged in accordance with a predetermined three-dimensional pattern and intended to perform, exclusively or together with other functions, an electronic function. The notion of topography of a semiconducting product refers to a series of related images, whichever way fixed or encoded, representing the three-dimensional pattern of the layers of which a semiconducting

169. Official Journal of the Republic of Serbia, n° 55/2013 and 66/2019.
170. *Ibid.*, n° 8/2014.
171. The Treaty is administered by the World Intellectual Property Organization.
172. As of 1 Dec. 2015.

product is composed and in which series, each image has the pattern or part of the pattern of a surface of the semiconducting product at any stage of its manufacture.[173]

280. Therefore, one should make a clear distinction between a semiconducting product and a topography (layout design) of integrated circuits which is being materialized through such products. Only the topographies, as immaterial goods, are being protected under intellectual property rules. It should also be clarified that the information contained in the integrated circuit is not subject matter of protection either. Where the topography consists of elements that are commonplace in the semiconductor industry, it shall be protected only to the extent that the combination of such elements, taken as a whole, fulfils the protection requirements prescribed by the law.

§3. Conditions of Protection

281. Under the Topographies of Semiconducting Products Act, only new layout designs of semiconducting products may be protected, provided that the protection is required within the prescribed deadline. A topography is deemed new if, taken as a whole, it does not represent a commonplace in the semiconductor industry (i.e., it is not well-known in the semiconductor industry). The fulfilment of the novelty criterion is assessed at the moment of the creation of a topography. This rule does not seem logical, given the fact that it departs from the general rules of interpretation of the novelty criterion in industrial property law and the fact that the exact moment of creation of a topography is very difficult, if not impossible, to determine, since it usually represents the trade secret of the company.[174] It should be clarified that the creation of topographies rarely consists of a 'pioneer work'. Instead, the creator combines the existing elements and/or adapts the existing topographies. Therefore, when concluding whether the novelty criterion is fulfilled, one should consider the topography as a whole, while neglecting the possible lack of novelty of some of its elements.

282. An application for the registration of a topography must be filed within the period of two years as from the date on which the first commercial exploitation of the topography has started anywhere in the world. Where a topography has not been commercially exploited anywhere in the world, an application must be filed within the period of fifteen years from its first fixation or encoding.[175]

---

173. *See* Topographies of Semiconducting Products Act, Art. 2.
174. *See* S. Marković, D. Popović, *supra,* 195–196.
175. *See* Topographies of Semiconducting Products Act, Art. 20.

§4. Formalities: Procedure for Obtaining Protection

283. Protection of topographies of semiconducting products is obtained by means of registration before the IP Office of the RS. The registration procedure is regulated under the Plant Breeders' Rights Act and the General Administrative Procedure Act.

I. Application for Topography of Semiconducting Products Registration

284. The procedure for the grant of the topography of semiconducting products right is initiated by filing an application for the registration of a topography before the IP Office.[176] The right to the topography of semiconducting products protection is vested in the topography creator, or his legal successor, or the employer in specific cases prescribed by the law.

285. The right to protection shall apply in favour of natural persons who are nationals of the RS or nationals of a Member State of the WTO or who have habitual residence on the territory of the RS or on the territory of a WTO Member State. Where a topography has been created in the course of the creator's employment or has been commissioned under a contract other than the employment contract, the right to protection shall apply in favour of natural persons who are nationals of the RS or nationals of a WTO Member State or who have their habitual residence on the territory of the RS or a WTO Member State, as well as in favour of legal persons who have their principal place of business on the territory of the RS or a WTO Member State. Foreign natural and legal persons not having their habitual residence or principal place of business on the territory of a WTO Member State may still enjoy protection where such treatment derives from international treaties signed by the RS. Where no right to protection exists in accordance with these criteria, the right to protection shall apply in favour of the persons who have first commercially exploited on the territory of the RS or on the territory of a WTO Member State a topography which has not previously been commercially exploited anywhere in the world, or in favour of the persons who have been exclusively authorized to commercially exploit the topography on the territory of the RS or on the territory of a WTO Member State by the person entitled to dispose of the topography. In proceedings before the IP Office, a foreign natural or legal person not having his/her principle place of business or habitual residence on the territory of the RS must be represented by a local attorney or agent registered within the IP Office.[177]

286. A written application for the registration of a topography is to be submitted to the IP Office. The application is to be filed in Serbian language. However, the use of special technical terms in English is allowed if such terms are used in the field of technology to which topography relates. In other cases, English terms may be used

176. *Ibid.*, Arts 16–25.
177. *Ibid.*, Arts 6–8.

in parallel with their Serbian translation. A separate application is to be filed for each individual topography. The mandatory elements of the application are:

– request for the grant of the right to a topography;
– documents identifying a topography;
– copy of semiconducting products manufactured according to the topography for which the protection is sought, if the integrated circuit has been commercially exploited;
– statement of the date of the first commercial exploitation of the topography, if that date is earlier than the filing date; and
– statement of entitlement to filing the application if the applicant is not the creator of the topography.

The applicant may request from the IP Office to treat some of the documents attached to the request for the grant of the right to a topography as a trade secret. Also, an application by a national of the RS with respect to a topography found to be important for the national defence or national security is considered to be confidential. The provisions of the Patent Act governing the protection of inventions, the disclosure of which would be detrimental to the national defence or national security shall apply by analogy to such topographies.

287. Once the application for the grant of the right to a topography is submitted and the procedural fees are paid, the IP Office examines the fulfilment of the above-mentioned formal requirements prescribed by the law.

II. Grant of Topography of Semiconducting Products Right

288. If the formal requirements that an application for the registration of a topography of semiconducting products must satisfy have been fulfilled, the IP Office shall issue a decision requesting the applicant to pay the registration fee, as well as the costs of topography publication, and submit the proof of payments made. The applicant may request that certain elements of topography are treated as confidential and remain unpublished. Following this step, the IP Office shall issue the decision on the registration of the topography of semiconducting products right, which will subsequently be entered into the Registry of protected topographies of semiconducting products. The right holder shall be issued a certificate. The grant of the topography of semiconducting products right is published in the Official Journal of the IP Office.

289. The right on a topography of semiconducting product shall therefore be granted without the fulfilment of novelty condition being verified. This rule significantly departs from general rules of industrial property law. However, a person claiming that the registered topography was not new at the moment of its creation may initiate annulment proceedings.

290. If the IP Office establishes that the application does not meet the registration requirements, it shall notify the applicant in writing of the reasons due to which a topography cannot be granted and invite the applicant to submit its observations. Where the applicant fails to respond, or where the applicant responds but the IP Office nevertheless considers that the topography of semiconducting product may not be registered, a decision on refusal of the registration shall be issued.

§5. Ownership and Transfer: Assignment – Licenses

291. Ownership of the rights granted with regard to the topography of semiconducting products belongs to the creator of the latter. Where several persons have jointly created a topography, they will jointly exercise the exclusive rights. Where a topography is created in the course of the creator's employment, the right to protection shall apply in favour of the creator's employer, unless otherwise provided by the employment contract. The provisions of the Patent Act regulating the legal regime of inventions created in the course of the inventor's employment apply *mutatis mutandis.* Where a topography is created under a contract other than a contract of employment, the right to protection shall apply in favour of a party to the contract by which the topography has been commissioned, unless otherwise stipulated. The right to protection also applies in favour of successors in title of the abovementioned persons.[178]

292. The rights granted with regard to topographies of semiconducting products may be assigned, licensed and pledged.[179] Exclusive right to topography may be, in whole or in part, subject of an assignment on the basis of an assignment contract, or a court/administrative decision. The assignment contract has to be concluded in writing. Assignment is to be recorded in the appropriate registry of the IP Office. Registration of the assignment produces effects with respect to third parties. Exclusive right to topography may also be licensed, in whole or in part, on the basis of a licence agreement, concluded in writing. Licensing is to be recorded in the appropriate registry of the IP Office. Registration of the licence agreement produces effects with respect to third parties. The rights granted with regard to topography of semiconducting products may be pledged. This may result from a contract, court decision or decision of another public authority. The agreement has to be concluded in written form and is to be recorded in the appropriate registry of the IP Office. The provisions of the Patent Act governing the assignment, licensing and pledge of patents shall apply *mutatis mutandis.* [180]

---

178. *Ibid.,* Art. 5.
179. *Ibid.,* Art. 15.
180. *See* S. Marković, D. Popović, *supra,* 212–216, 235–243.

§6. SCOPE OF EXCLUSIVE RIGHTS

293. A registered topography of semiconducting products confers to its holder the exclusive right to use it and to prevent any third party not having his consent from using it. The aforementioned use covers, in particular, the reproduction of the protected topography as a whole or its essential parts, in any manner and in any form, as well as the commercial exploitation or importing of the topography or the semiconducting product containing protected topography or the products incorporating the semiconducting product. The right holder is also entitled to mark a semiconducting product produced by using the protected topography with a capital letter 'T'.[181]

§7. EXCEPTIONS AND LIMITATIONS TO TOPOGRAPHIES OF SEMICONDUCTING PRODUCT PROTECTION

294. The Topographies of Semiconducting Products Act prescribes several limitations to exclusive protection of a registered topography.[182] Rights conferred by a registered topography of semiconducting product cannot be exercised in respect of acts of reproduction of a topography for personal use intended for non-commercial purposes, as well as acts of reproduction of a topography for the purpose of analysing, evaluating or teaching the concepts, processes, systems or techniques embodied in the topography or the topography itself.

295. Further to these two exceptions, the Serbian legislator prescribed a specific limitation of the exclusive right to topography of semiconducting product, usually referred to as 'reverse engineering'. Namely, the law authorizes the creation of a new topography by means of analysis or research of another, already protected topography. If such acts would be undertaken with respect to other protected intellectual goods (e.g., patented inventions), they would represent acts of infringement of exclusive intellectual property rights.[183]

296. The classical doctrine of exhaustion of intellectual property rights applies to topographies of semiconducting products rights as well. The rights conferred by a registered topography shall not extend to acts relating to a product in which a topography included within the scope of protection of the registered design is incorporated, when the product has been put on the market in the RS by the holder of the topography of semiconducting products right or with his consent.

181. *See* Topographies of Semiconducting Products Act, Arts 9, 14.
182. *Ibid.*, Arts 10–11.
183. *See* S. Marković, D. Popović, *supra,* 199–200.

§8. Duration of Protection

297. A topography which meets the requirements prescribed by the Topographies of Semiconducting Products Act is protected, upon registration by the IP Office, for a period of ten years as of from the date of the filing of the application or from the day when the topography was first commercially exploited anywhere in the world.[184] Contrary to general rules of industrial property law and similarly to the rules on duration of copyright, the exclusive rights to topography of semiconducting products come to an end upon the expiry of the calendar year in which a ten years period has lapsed.

298. The IP Office may revoke at any time its decision to grant the exclusive right at the request of any interested party, if it establishes that:

- the subject matter of protection was not a topography within the meaning of the Act;
- the topography did not meet the protection requirements;
- the application was not filed within the prescribed time limits;
- the right holder is not entitled to protection within the meaning of the Act and/or that he did not have a representative in proceedings before the IP Office; and
- the documents submitted with the application do not have the prescribed content.[185]

Decision to revoke the topography shall not produce any effect on court decisions determining the existence of infringements of exclusive rights, which were legally binding at the moment of the adoption of the decision to revoke the topography, nor on assignment and licensing agreements that have been entered into, if, and to the extent that, such agreements have been executed, provided the plaintiff/ right holder has acted in good faith.

§9. Infringement and Remedies

299. The infringement of the exclusive rights of the owner of topography of semiconducting products results in civil and criminal remedies. Civil remedies are regulated under the Topographies of Semiconducting Products Act.[186] They consist of the indemnification of any damages caused by the infringement of the right to topography of semiconducting product. The amount of such compensation is determined with regard to the usual licence fee the right owner would receive for the use of a protected topography. The provisions of the Patent Act governing the civil law protection of a patented invention shall apply by analogy to the civil law protection of the protected topography of semiconducting product. However, a person who, at the moment of the acquisition of a semiconducting products, does not know or has

184. *See* Topographies of Semiconducting Products Act, Arts 12–13.
185. *Ibid.*, Art. 28.
186. *Ibid.*, Art. 32.

no reasonable grounds to believe that the product is protected by an exclusive right and shall not be liable for a civil law infringement of the exclusive right to a topography. But, the court may, at the request of the right holder, require from such a person the payment of remuneration for the commercial exploitation of the protected topography, from the moment the person learned or had reasonable grounds to believe that the topography is protected.

300. Further to civil law responsibility for violation of a protected topography, the Topographies of Semiconducting Products Act lists certain types of conduct that are subject to (pseudo) criminal penalties.[187] Namely, a corporation or any other legal person who violates a protected topography of semiconducting product is sanctioned on grounds of corporate offence (in Serbian, *privredni prestup*) by a fine. A responsible person in a legal entity who is found to infringe the exclusive rights to topography may also be fined. The court may also undertake precautionary measures and/or order the publication of the judgment, pursuant to general rules on corporate offences. A natural person who infringes the exclusive rights to topography shall be fined on grounds of misdemeanour. The infringing objects in a misdemeanour and the objects used for perpetration of the misdemeanour may be forfeited and the infringing objects may be destroyed. Finally, a legal person who acts as representative in the exercising of the rights under the Topographies of Semiconducting Products Act without a power of attorney may be sanctioned on grounds of misdemeanour by a fine. The responsible person in a legal entity may also be fined.

§10. Overlapping and Relation to Other Intellectual Property Rights

301. The Topographies of Semiconducting Products Act does not lay down any rule regarding the overlapping of the exclusive protection of topographies and other intellectual property rights. Under general IP rules, the parallel protection of an intellectual good by two different intellectual property rights is *a priori* possible, provided that the protection requirements are fulfilled. However, given the specific characteristics of topographies of semiconducting products, it is not likely that the requirements for a different type of protection would be met.

187. *Ibid.*, Arts 33–35.

Chapter 9. Trade Secrets

§1. Sources – Legislation

302. Until 2011, there was no specific statute enacted in Serbia for purposes of trade secrets protection. Rights as to such secrets and confidential information resulted from various statutory rules and were included in different branches of law. Presently, the general legal regime on trade secrets and confidential information is prescribed by the Act on the protection of trade secrets (hereinafter, the Trade Secrets Act), which was enacted in 2021.[188] However, trade secrets legal regime continues to be partly regulated by numerous other acts, such as the Act on the capital market,[189] Patent Act,[190] Industrial Design Act,[191] Act on investment funds,[192] Banking Act,[193] Bankruptcy Act,[194] Labor and Employment Act[195] and Companies Act.[196] The Trade Secrets Act does not limit the protection of trade secrets and confidential information resulting from other legal sources. The case law in this area is very limited and reflects the lack of litigation in Serbia with regard to trade secrets. Finally, the Penal Code prescribes criminal responsibility for disclosing a business secret.[197]

§2. Protection of Trade Secrets

303. The Trade Secrets Act regulates the protection of trade secrets and confidential information against all acts of unfair competition. The Trade Secrets Act defines a trade secret as any information which meets the following three requirements: (1) the information is secret because it is not known to the public, entirely or with respect to its structure or its components, or it is easily available to persons who, within their activities, usually get into contact with such type of information; (2) the information which has a commercial value due to its non-public character; and (3) a person who lawfully controls the information has undertaken reasonable measures in order to secure its confidentiality.[198] The information that has been denoted as a trade secret for the sake of covering a criminal act, abuse of discretion or abuse of official position or any other illegal act shall not be protected under the Trade Secrets Act. If certain information is specifically marked as not representing

188. Official Journal of the Republic of Serbia, n° 53/21.
189. *Ibid.*, n° 31/2011, 112/2015, 108/2016, 9/2020 and 153/2020.
190. *Ibid.*, n° 99/2011, 113/2017, 95/2018 and 66/2019.
191. *Ibid.*, n° 104/2009, 45/2015 and 44/2018.
192. *Ibid.*, n° 73/2019.
193. *Ibid.*, n° 107/2005, 91/2010 and 14/2015.
194. *Ibid.*, n° 104/2009, 99/2011, 71/2012, 83/2014, 113/2017, 44/2018 and 95/2018.
195. *Ibid.*, n° 24/2005, 61/2005, 54/2009, 32/2013, 75/2014, 13/2017, 113/2017 and 95/2018.
196. *Ibid.*, n° 36/2011, 99/2011, 83/2014, 5/2015, 44/2018, 95/2018 i 91/2019.
197. *Ibid.*, n° 85/2005, 88/2005, 107/2005, 72/2009, 111/2009, 121/2009, 104/2013, 108/2014, 94/2016 and 35/2019.
198. *See* Trade Secrets Act, Art. 2.

a trade secret and/or confidential information under any *lex specialis,* such information shall not enjoy protection under the Trade Secrets Act either. The right to protect trade secrets under the Trade Secrets Act is recognized to any Serbian or foreign natural or legal person. Any person legally controlling the use of a trade secret is considered to be the holder of a trade secret within the meaning of the Trade Secrets Act. The protection of a trade secret lasts as long as the information representing the trade secret is being kept confidential.

304. Undisclosed test data or other data whose creation require certain effort and investment, filed to the government bodies with a view to getting permission to market the medicines or medical devices or agricultural chemical products that use new chemical components, or biocide products shall enjoy protection as trade secrets. Also, a trade secret is considered to be any other data proclaimed as such by a specific statutory act, other regulation or act of a corporation.

305. The information representing a trade secret may be acquired, used and disclosed legally and illegally. The transfer of the right to use a trade secret shall be considered legal if it has been performed with the consent of the trade secret holder. Exceptionally, a trade secret may be disclosed/transferred legally even without the consent of the holder, if such disclosure/transfer has been undertaken in accordance with a specific statutory act and in a way not contrary to fair business practices. If a dispute with respect to the use of a trade secret arises, a person claiming to have legally acquired such confidential information has to prove it. On the other hand, any action undertaken within the framework of industrial or commercial activities which results in the disclosure, acquisition or utilization by other persons of the information representing a trade secret, without the authorization of its holder and in a manner contrary to the law and fair business practices, is considered to be an act of unfair competition. An act of unfair competition is considered to be any action which causes damage to a competitor or another natural or legal person, in particular:

- breach of contract;
- misuse of trust;
- industrial or commercial espionage;
- fraud;
- solicitation to any of the abovementioned acts; and
- acquisition of information which are considered to be trade secrets by persons who were aware or had an obligation to be aware of the fact that these information are considered trade secrets and that they have been obtained by one of the abovementioned acts.[199]

Exceptionally, the protected information may be disclosed if the authority competent for issuing a licence for the marketing of medicines or medical devices or agricultural chemical products that use new chemical components, or biocide products establishes that such disclosure is necessary for the protection of the public

199. *Ibid.,* Arts 3–4.

interest. Such disclosure may also result from a decision adopted by the special authority in charge of providing the access to information of public interest. Further to this, test data or other data whose creation require certain effort and investment, filed to the government bodies with a view to getting permission to market the medicines or medical devices or agricultural chemical products that use new chemical components, or biocide products may be disclosed if the measures have been undertaken which ensure that the data are protected from unfair commercial use, or the holder of a trade secret expressly permits in writing their disclosure for commercial bona fide use.

§3. Infringement and Remedies

306. The protection of a trade secret is prescribed under the Trade Secrets Act. In case of infringement of a trade secret, its holder may initiate civil law proceedings and request the termination of all acts that may lead to illegal acquisition, utilization or disclosure of the trade secret and the prohibition of the illegal acquisition, utilization or disclosure of data which represent a trade secret. The plaintiff may also request:

- prevention of entering the channels of commerce and/or seizure and withdrawal from the channels of commerce, alteration or destruction of all objects containing data which represent trade secret, if such data can be seen or transferred directly or indirectly;
- compensation of damages, including the actual damage and the lost profits;
- exclusion of the infringer from the corporation, is he/she is a member of the corporation;
- termination of employment, if the infringer has been employed by a legal person; and
- publication of sentence in the media at the expense of the defendant.

When reaching a decision, the court will particularly consider the balance between the seriousness of the violation and the interests of third parties.

307. The complaint for infringement of a trade secret may be filed within one year following the day the plaintiff has become aware of the infringement and the infringer, but not later than within five years following the day when infringement was committed. The court may order an interim measure at the request of the person who makes it credible that the trade secret he legally controls has been violated, or that such violation is imminent. The interim measure may consist in the seizure or withdrawal from circulation of all objects containing the trade secret or resulting in the violation of the trade secret, all means for the production of these objects, or the court may pass the measure of prohibition of actions initiating the violation or enabling the violation of the trade secret. Further to this type of interim measure, the court may also comply with the request of the person who makes it credible that the trade secret been violated, or that such violation is imminent, or that there is a reasonable suspicion that evidence will be destroyed or that it will not be possible to collect it later, to order an interim measure to secure evidence without giving prior notice to, or hearing the person from whom the evidence is to be collected. The securing of evidence is being realized through the inspection of premises, vehicles, books, documents, as well as the seizure of documents, blocking of bank accounts, confiscation of cash and stocks, questioning of witnesses and expert witnesses. Both types of measures may be requested even before filing a complaint, provided that subsequently a complaint is filed within thirty days from the date of rendering the decision on interim measure. The alleged infringer of the trade secret may request from the court to set, at the expense of the plaintiff, an indemnity payable in case the request is found not to be grounded.

308. Further to civil law responsibility for violation of a trade secret, the Trade Secrets Act lists certain types of conduct that are subject to (pseudo) criminal penalties. Namely, a corporation or any other legal person who violates a trade secret is sanctioned on grounds of corporate offence (in Serbian, *privredni prestup*) by a fine. A responsible person in a legal entity who is found to infringe industrial design right may also be fined. The infringing objects and the objects used for the perpetration of the corporate offence may be forfeited and the infringing objects may be destroyed.[200]

309. Finally, the Penal Code prescribes criminal responsibility for disclosing a business secret. A person who without authorization communicates to another, hands over or in any other way makes available information representing a business secret or who obtains such information with the intention of handing it over to an unauthorized person shall be punished by imprisonment of three months to five years. If the offence is committed for gain, the offender shall be punished by imprisonment of two to ten years.[201]

200. *Ibid.*, Art. 21.
201. *See* Penal Code, Art. 240.

Chapter 10. Geographical Indications and Designations of Origin

§1. Sources – Legislation

310. The Act on the protection of indications of geographical origin (hereinafter, the Indications of Geographical Origin Act)[202] is the main source of rules governing the protection of designations of origin and geographical indications (GIs) in Serbia. With respect to the registration procedure, the Government adopted the Regulation on the contents of the application for registration of indications of geographical origin, and the contents of the request for recognition of the status of the authorized user of indications of geographical origin.[203] National rules on the protection of designations of origin and GIs are harmonized with the European Union law; thus Serbian legislator accepted the EU terminology and concept when defining the subject matter of protection.

311. Serbia acceded to main sources of international intellectual property law governing the protection of indications of geographical origin. The Federal Republic of Yugoslavia, which Serbia was a part of, became party to the Lisbon Agreement for the Protection of Appellations of Origin and their International Registration on 1 March 1999.[204] Following the dissolution of the Union of Serbia and Montenegro, Serbia submitted to WIPO a Declaration of continued application on 19 September 2006. Further to joining the Lisbon Agreement, the Federal Republic of Yugoslavia, which Serbia was a part of, acceded to the Madrid Agreement for the Repression of False or Deceptive Indications of Source on Goods on 18 February 2000.[205] In 2006, following the dissolution of the Union of Serbia and Montenegro, Serbia submitted to WIPO the abovementioned Declaration of continued application.

312. Further to protection of indications of geographical origin under specific rules of industrial property law, such indications may also be protected under unfair competition rules and under trademark law (as collective trademarks).

§2. Subject Matter of Protection

313. Under the Indications of Geographical Origin Act, the notion of indications of geographical origin encompasses designations of origin and GIs.[206] A designation of origin (DO) (in Serbian, *ime porekla*) is defined as a geographical name of a region, locality or country used to designate a product originating therein, the quality and specific characteristics of which are exclusively or essentially due to a

202. Official Journal of the Republic of Serbia, n° 18/2010.
203. *Ibid.*, n° 93/2010.
204. Official Journal of the Republic of Yugoslavia – International Agreements, n° 6/1998. FR Yugoslavia acceded to the Stockholm Act (1967).
205. Official Journal of the Republic of Yugoslavia – International Agreements, n° 1/1999. FR Yugoslavia acceded to the Lisbon Act (1958) and the Additional Act of Stockholm (1967).
206. *See* Indications of Geographical Origin Act, Arts 3–4.

particular geographical environment with its inherent natural and human factors, and which is produced, processed and prepared entirely within a defined geographical area. On the other hand, a GI (in Serbian, *geografska oznaka*) is defined as a name which identifies particular goods as goods originating from the territory of specific country, region or locality within such territory, where a given quality, reputation or other characteristics of such goods can be essentially attributed to their geographical origin, and the production and/or processing and/or preparation of which take place in the defined geographical area. These definitions represent a reception into Serbian law of Article 5 of the EU Regulation on quality schemes for agricultural products and foodstuffs.[207]

314. Exceptionally, an indication of geographical origin may also be a name which is not a GI of a country, region or locality, if such indication has become well known through long-standing use in trade as a traditional name of product originating in that area, or a historical name of such area, provided that other requirements for a DO or GI protection are met. Where the names of two or more places of origin of the product are identical or nearly identical in written or pronounced form (homonymic names), protection of such geographical names shall be granted to all interested persons meeting the requirements prescribed by the law, based on the principles of fair and equal treatment of producers on the market and of truthful consumer information, except where this may mislead the public as to the true geographical origin of the product.[208]

315. Indications of geographical origin may be used not only to mark the agricultural products and foodstuffs, but also to label industrial products and traditional handicrafts products and services. However, the Indications of Geographical Origin Act does not govern the registration of indications used for wine and brandy (in Serbian, *rakija*). The registration of indications applied to wine and brandy is regulated under separate acts – Act on wines[209] and Act on brandies and other spirits.[210]

§3. Conditions of Protection

316. In order to be protected, indications of geographical origin must not be contrary to public order or accepted principles of morality, must not represent a name of protected plant varieties or animal species, must not mislead consumers as to the nature, origin, quality, manner of production or other characteristics of the product, must not be identical or similar to a registered trademark, must not represent a generic name. Further to this, names that are exact names of a geographical locality cannot be registered if they cause false impression among consumers that the product originates from another locality. Finally, as it may be concluded from the definitions of a DO and GI, there should be a causal link between the characteristics of

207. Official Journal of the European Union, n° L343/1 of 14 Dec. 2012.
208. *See* Indications of Geographical Origin Act, Arts 5–6.
209. Official Journal of the Republic of Serbia, n° 41/2009 and 93/2012.
210. *Ibid.*, n° 41/2009.

a product and characteristics of the geographical locality where such product is made.[211] These conditions shall be explained in more detail.

317. Under the first criterion, the publication or use of a geographic name must not be contrary to public order or the accepted principles of morality. Normally, this requirement is always met, since it is very difficult to imagine that the name of a geographic locality, which would serve as a protected indication of origin, would be contrary to public morality or order. However, in case a geographical locality is named after a saint, for example, it could be arguable whether such an indication should be used to designate a product in the course of trade. Given the fact that, contrary to a trademark registrant, an indication of GI registrant cannot choose the indication it wishes to protect, the IP Office should be less restrictive when assessing the fulfilment of this condition.

318. The name of protected plant varieties or animal species may not be registered as an indication of geographical origin if this could mislead consumers as to the true origin of product. The legislator had in mind those names of plant varieties and national species that have a geographical reference as a part of its name (e.g., Amsterdam rose). The persons cultivating such species anywhere in the world must be allowed to use the variety/species name without any restrictions.

319. Names that may mislead consumers as to the nature, origin, quality, manner of production or other characteristics of the product cannot be protected as indications of geographical origin. Also, names that are identical or similar to previously registered trademarks cannot be protected if, in view of the reputation, renown and long-standing use of such trademarks, they may mislead consumers as to the origin of such product. However, if an indication of geographical origin is registered although it is identical or similar to a previously registered trademark, the trademark owner may continue using its trademark, provided the latter was registered in good faith.[212]

320. Indications that are exact names of the country, region or locality of origin of the products cannot be registered if they cause false impression among consumers that the product originates from another country, region or locality. This rule serves to prevent the registration of toponyms which exist in different countries, even different parts of the world. For example, a registration of an indication of geographical origin containing the toponym 'Paris' in relation to products originating from Paris, USA would be misleading, since the consumers would wrongfully associate the products to the more famous toponym – the French capital city.

321. Under the Indications of Geographical Origin Act, it is not possible to protect indications which have become generic, due to their long-standing use. Generic names are names usually employed to designate a certain product/category of products.

211. *Ibid.*, Arts 3–4, 8.
212. *Ibid.*, Art. 58.

322. A foreign indication of origin may be registered in Serbia only if it is protected and used in its country of origin. The registration of foreign indications of geographical origin is being conducted pursuant to multilateral or bilateral international agreements which Serbia is a party to.

323. Finally, as it may be concluded from the definitions of designations of origin and GIs, there must be a causal link between the characteristics of a product and characteristics of the geographical locality where such product is made. These characteristics of the geographical locality may include human and/or natural factors. Human factors, such as the traditional manner of preparation of a product, and/or natural factors, such as the climate, should influence the characteristic of a specific product which is going to be labelled by the protected indication of geographical origin. If the influence of such factors on the characteristics of a product is significant, the product concerned shall be marked by a DO. If the influence is less determining, the product may be labelled by a GI. Exceptionally, a product that possesses a proven traditional feature, that is of high repute and is well known may be protected by a DO[213] even where raw material for the production of such products originates from an area different from or broader than the processing area, provided that the production area is limited and that special requirements for producing such raw material are in place, as well as an inspection system ensuring supervision of fulfilment of such special conditions.[214]

§4. Formalities: Procedure for Obtaining Protection

324. Protection of designations of origin and GIs is obtained by means of registration before the IP Office of the RS. The procedure of registration of indications of geographical origin applied to wines and brandies is conducted before the Ministry of Agriculture and is regulated under sector-specific rules.

325. The registration procedure is organized into two phases. In the first phase, the IP Office examines the application for registration of a DO or GI. If the requirements prescribed by the law are met, the IP Office registers the indication. At the end of the first phase of the registration procedure, the indication of geographical origin is recognized, but the subjective exclusive right with respect to the indication has not yet been established since no one is being authorized to use the registered indication of geographical origin. It is only in the second phase of the procedure that such an exclusive right is being recognized. The second phase therefore consists in examination of fulfilment of conditions for the recognition of the status of an authorized user of the protected indication of geographical origin.[215]

213. This rule does not apply to geographical indications.
214. *See* Indications of Geographical Origin Act, Art. 7.
215. *See* S. Marković, D. Popović, *supra,* 178–181.

I. Registration of an Indication of Geographical Origin

326. The procedure of registration of an indication of geographical origin is initiated by a registration application submitted to the IP Office.[216] The applications may be filed by:

- national natural or legal persons who, within a specified geographical area, produce the products that are designated by the name of such geographical area;
- associations of such persons, chambers of commerce, associations of consumers and state authorities that are, within their regular activities, interested in the protection of indications of geographical origin; and
- foreign natural or legal persons or foreign associations, provided that the indication of geographical origin is recognized in its country of origin, and provided that the right to submit the application in Serbia results from international agreements.

Foreign natural and legal persons must be represented by a local attorney or agent registered within the IP Office. One application may contain the request for registration of only one indication of geographical origin and may refer to only one type of product. The application must contain the formal request for registration of an indication of geographical origin, description of the geographical area, and data on specific characteristics of the product which is going to be labelled with the indication.

327. The formal request for registration must contain the following elements: name and address of the applicant, GI to be protected, type of product to be designated by a GI, geographical name of the area or place of origin of the product to be designated by a specific geographical name, designation of the authorized certification body performing product quality control and control of the specific characteristics of those products, proof of payment of the prescribed fee. Where an applicant is a foreign natural or legal person or an association, the request has to be accompanied by a document issued by a competent authority in the country of origin verifying that such indication of geographical origin is recognized in the country of origin.

328. Each application has to contain data on specific characteristics of the product which is going to be designated with the indication of geographical origin. If the application is submitted in view of the registration of a GI, such data should be submitted in the form of specification describing the manner of production, designating the specific characteristics or qualities of the product, or indicating the data on reputation of the product, explaining the link between the qualities or reputation or other product characteristics and the described geographical area, providing the proof that the product originates from the described geographical area, and explaining the method of labelling of the product. If specific characteristics of a product

216. *See* Indications of Geographical Origin Act, Arts 18–30.

are related to the quality or other specific features of the product, the specification has to be accompanied by a certificate issued by authorized certification organization.

329. Therefore, an applicant needs to indicate which certification body is in charge of performing the product quality control and control of the specific characteristics of a product. The quality control should be understood as the verification of whether the quality and the specific characteristics of the product, the method of production and the origin of the raw material are in compliance with the data indicated in the study or specification submitted to the IP Office. A certification organization has to be accredited by the National accreditation body. In case of the quality control of agricultural products and foodstuffs, a certification body has to be authorized by the Ministry of Agriculture and accredited by the National accreditation body.

330. On the other hand, if the application is submitted in view of the registration of a DO, data on specific characteristics of the product should be submitted in the form of a study containing information on customary manner and method of production of such product, data on specific characteristics and qualities of the product, explanation of the causal relationship between the specific characteristics and qualities of the product and the described geographical area, as well as proof that the product originates from the described geographical area, proof that the raw material control has been performed, data on the method of labelling of the product, and data on quantity of the product produced in one year. The study has to be accompanied by a certificate confirming that control of the quality and specific characteristics of the product has been performed.

331. An important element of the application is a description of the geographical area. Such description should include a detailed definition of boundaries of the area, geographical map, and information on geographical and human factors generating the specific characteristics, qualities or reputation of the relevant product. The applicant is supposed to define the boundaries of the relevant geographical area by reference to settlements and natural geographical objects, such as mountains, rivers, mountain ranges and other, which would enable a precise delineation from other geographical areas.

332. An application for registration of a DO or a GI shall be entered into the Registry of applications, kept by the IP Office, provided it contains all the mandatory elements prescribed by the Indications of Geographical Origin Act. If this is not the case, the IP Office shall invite the applicant to correct the deficiencies within the time period specified. If the applicant does not correct such deficiencies, the IP Office shall reject the application. Following the formal examination of an application, the IP Office shall proceed to examining the fulfilment of substantial conditions prescribed by the law. These conditions differ to a certain extent depending on whether the applicant aims at registering a DO or a GI. This distinction results from the 'intensity' of the causal link existing between the characteristics of the product which will be designated by an indication of geographical origin and the characteristics of the relevant geographical area. As already explained, this link is much more emphasized within the products that are to be marked with a protected DO.[217]

333. In the course of examination of substantive requirements for registration of an indication of geographical origin, the IP Office is required to obtain the formal opinion from the ministry generally competent for the activities relating to products/services which would be designated by such an indication. The competent ministry (usually the Ministry of Trade or the Ministry of Agriculture) is required to deliver such an opinion within two months from the day it was requested. The failure by the competent ministry to deliver such an opinion within the prescribed time frame does not however prevent the IP Office from continuing the registration procedure. The IP Office shall not require the opinion of the competent ministry if the application for registration is submitted under the Lisbon Agreement.

334. If the competent ministry has provided a positive opinion on fulfilment of registration requirements or if it has failed to provide an opinion, the IP Office shall continue with the registration procedure by verifying the fulfilment of substantive requirements prescribed by the Indications of Geographical Origin Act. Where the IP Office finds that such requirements are met, it shall issue a decision on registration of a DO or a GI and enter such indication into the Registry of indications of geographical origin. The registered indication of geographical origin, the information on the relevant geographical area and on the type of product to be marked are all published in the Official Journal of the IP Office.

335. If the competent ministry has provided a negative opinion on fulfilment of registration requirements and/or if the IP Office finds that the application fails to meet the requirements prescribed by the law, it shall notify the applicant in writing of the reasons for denial of registration and invite it to submit the observations within two months. Upon the applicant's substantiated request, the IP Office may extend the deadline for submitting the observations. Following the receipt of the applicant's observations, the IP Office shall request an opinion from the ministry competent for the activities relating to products/services which would be designated by such an indication. The failure by the competent ministry to deliver such an opinion within the prescribed time frame does not however prevent the IP Office from continuing the procedure. If the applicant fails to submit its observations or if, following the receipt of the applicant's observations, the IP Office still considers that the registration requirements are not met, it shall deny registration of the indication of geographical origin concerned. The decision on denial of registration may be appealed before the Government of Serbia within fifteen days from the day of the receipt of such a decision. The Government decision on appeal may be subject to administrative dispute before the Administrative Court.

336. As long as the registration proceedings are pending, the IP Office may, upon the applicant's request, convert the application for registration of a DO into an

217. *See* S. Marković, D. Popović, *supra,* 176–177.

application for registration of GI, and vice versa. The converted application shall keep the filing date of the initially filed application. The applicant wishing to convert the application submitted to the IP Office is required to pay a specific conversion fee.[218]

II. Recognition of an Authorized User Status

337. Once the indication of geographical origin is registered, the IP Office may proceed to examining whether the requirements for the recognition of the status of authorized user of such indication are met. This examination is conducted in the second phase of the registration proceedings and has to be initiated by a person interested in becoming an authorized user of a registered DO or GI. The status of the authorized user can be granted to any natural or legal person, as well as to associations of such persons if, on the specific geographical area, they produce the products which are named after the area and which possess the quality, specific characteristics or reputation due to that defined geographical area.

338. The procedure is initiated by filing an application for the recognition of status of an authorized user of a registered indication of geographical area before the IP Office of the RS.[219] The mandatory elements of the application are: the formal request for recognition of the status of authorized user, the proof of particular business activity performed within the defined geographical area, and the proof of product quality control performed by an authorized certification body listed in the application for registration of DO/GI.

339. The formal request for recognition of status of authorized user contains the name and address of the applicant, indication of the geographical name to be protected, indication of the type of product to be marked by the geographical name, name of area or place of origin of the product, explanation on the manner in which the product shall be marked, designation of specific characteristics of the product, and the proof of payment of the prescribed fee. The applicant is also required to submit the proof of conducting the specific business activity within the defined geographical area. The IP Office shall accept any appropriate certificate or decision issued by a competent authority as such a proof. Finally, the applicant needs to submit the proof of product quality control performed by an authorized certification body listed in the application for registration of DO/GI. This certificate must be issued within the period of three months prior to the initiation of the recognition procedure.

340. An application for recognition of status of authorized user of the registered DO or GI shall be entered into the Registry of applications, kept by the IP Office, provided it contains all the mandatory elements prescribed by the Indications of

218. *See* Indications of Geographical Origin Act, Art. 29.
219. *See* Indications of Geographical Origin Act, Arts 32–51.

Geographical Origin Act. If this is not the case, the IP Office shall invite the applicant to correct the deficiencies within the time period specified. If the applicant does not correct such deficiencies, the IP Office shall reject the application. In this area of industrial property law, the priority right is not as important as it is usually the case with respect to other industrial property rights, since all persons meeting the prescribed requirements shall be recognized the status of authorized user of an indication of geographical origin. Every authorized user has to tolerate the use of the registered indication of geographical origin by other authorized users. Therefore, a producer that was the first to submit the application for recognition of status of authorized user shall in no way be favoured. The number of authorized users per one indication of geographical origin is not limited by the law.

341. If the application for recognition of status of authorized user meets the formal requirements prescribed by the Indications of Geographical Origin Act, the IP Office shall proceed to examining the fulfilment of substantive conditions. In the course of examination of substantive requirements, the IP Office is required to obtain the formal opinion from the ministry generally competent for the activities relating to products/services which would be designated by such an indication. The competent ministry is required to deliver such an opinion within two months from the day it was requested. The failure by the competent ministry to deliver such an opinion within the prescribed time frame does not however prevent the IP Office from continuing the procedure.

342. If the application for recognition of status of authorized user of a DO or GI meets the substantive requirements prescribed by the Indications of Geographical Origin Act, the IP Office shall invite the applicant to pay the fee for recognition of such status for the first three years, as well as the costs of publication of information on the authorized user in the Official Journal of the IP Office, and to furnish the proof of payments made. Following this step, the IP Office shall issue a decision on recognition of status of authorized user, enter the data on the user and indication of origin in the Registry of authorized users kept by the IP Office, publish these data in the Official Journal of the Office and issue a certificate verifying the status of authorized user.

343. If, on the other hand, the ministry in charge of activities related to products/services which would be designated by an indication of geographical origin concerned delivered a negative opinion on the fulfilment of requirements for recognition of status of authorized user and/or if the IP Office finds that such requirements are not met, it shall notify the applicant in writing of the reasons for denial of registration and invite him to submit the observations within two months. Upon the applicant's substantiated request, the IP Office may extend the deadline for submitting the observations. Following the receipt of the applicant's observations, the IP Office shall request an opinion from the ministry competent for the activities relating to products/services which would be designated by such an indication. The failure by the competent ministry to deliver such an opinion within the prescribed time frame does not however prevent the IP Office from continuing the procedure. If the applicant fails to submit his observations or if, following the receipt of the applicant's observations, the IP Office still considers that the registration requirements are not met, it shall deny registration of the status of authorized user. The decision on denial of registration may be appealed before the Government of Serbia within fifteen days from the day of the receipt of such a decision. The Government decision on appeal may be subject to administrative dispute before the Administrative Court.

344. While the registration proceedings are pending, the IP Office may, upon the applicant's request, convert the application for recognition of status of authorized user of a DO into an application for recognition of status of authorized user of GI, and vice versa. The converted application shall keep the filing date of the initially filed application. The applicant wishing to convert the application submitted to the IP Office is required to pay a specific conversion fee. The request for conversion of status of authorized user may be submitted to the IP Office provided that, in the course of proceedings for registration of a DO or GI, a request for conversion of application for registration of an indication has also been submitted.

§5. Ownership and Transfer: Assignment – Licenses

345. A registered DO or registered GI may be used only by persons who were recognized the status of authorized user of such DO/GI, and which were entered in the Registry kept by the IP Office. The number of authorized user per one DO/GI is not limited.

346. A registered DO or registered GI cannot be subject to agreements on assignment of rights, licence, or pledge. Furthermore, if a registered DO or registered GI is the subject matter of a registered trademark or an application for trademark registration, such trademark cannot be assigned, licensed, pledged or the like.[220] The prohibition of transfer of rights should be understood in the context of a generally unrestricted access of interested producers to the status of authorized user of a registered DO/GI, provided they fulfil the conditions prescribed in an objective, non-discriminatory manner.

§6. Scope of Exclusive Rights

347. Every authorized user of a registered DO or a registered GI has the right to mark its products with a sign 'controlled designation of origin' or 'controlled GI'. The authorized user has to tolerate that other authorized users of the same indication of geographical origin also mark their products using the same indication. The aforementioned use also covers the use of an indication on packaging, catalogues, brochures, advertisements, posters and other forms of offer, on instructions, invoices, in business correspondence and other forms of business documentation, as well as for the purpose of imports and exports of products bearing such indication

220. *See* Indications of Geographical Origin Act, Art. 60.

of geographical origin.[221] Persons who do not have the status of authorized user of a registered indication are not allowed to:

- use the registered DO or registered GI in respect of products not covered by the registration insofar as such products are similar to the products registered under that indication or insofar as such use hinders the reputation of the protected indication of geographical origin;
- make copies or counterfeit the registered indication of geographical origin, as well as to use its translation, transcription or transliteration even if such indication is supplemented with the words 'kind', 'type', 'method', 'imitation', 'as produced in' and the like, even where true geographical origin of the product is given;
- use the false or misleading indication as to the provenance, origin, nature or quality of the product, on the packaging, advertising material or documents, liable to cause confusion with respect to the origin of the product; and
- perform any other acts liable to cause confusion in the course of trade concerning the true origin of the products.[222]

Persons who do not have the status of the authorized user of the registered DO or registered GI are not allowed to use a trademark consisting of the sign which is identical or similar to the indication of geographical origin registered on the level of the European Union in compliance with the EU law, which refers to similar products that do not fulfil the conditions for the use of the indication of geographical origin.

§7. Exceptions and Limitations to Indications of Geographical Origin Protection

348. The Indications of Geographical Origin Act does not lay down specific provisions on exceptions and limitations to exclusive rights on a registered DO/GIs. However, as already explained, every authorized user of a registered DO/GI must tolerate that other authorized users use the same indication to label their products. Furthermore, in certain situations, the holder of a registered indication of geographical origin must tolerate the use of the same indication by a trademark owner or by a person exercising his/her personal rights.[223]

221. *Ibid.,* Art. 56.
222. *Ibid.,* Art. 57.
223. *See* § 10 of the present chapter.

§8. Duration of Protection

349. Duration of protection of a registered DO and a registered GI is not limited.[224] Therefore, such indications of geographical origin shall be protected as long as the protection requirements are met and the prescribed fees are paid.

350. In case of the protection in Serbia of a foreign indication of geographical origin, the protection shall cease to be valid if protection in the country of origin should terminate. The IP Office shall issue a decision on termination of validity of a foreign DO/GI registered in Serbia, at the request of the interested party that submits a certificate issued by the competent authority in the country of origin confirming that the protection in the country of origin ceased, or on receiving a notification directly from the competent authority of the country of origin.[225] A decision on termination of protection of a foreign DO/GI may be appealed before the Government of Serbia within fifteen days from the day of the receipt of such a decision. The Government decision on appeal may be subject to administrative dispute before the Administrative Court.

351. The protection of registered GI may terminate if the latter has become a generic name. A registered DO cannot become generic; therefore, this manner of termination of protection applies only to GIs. The court proceedings aiming at establishing that a registered GI has become generic may be initiated by any interested party. The protection of a GI shall cease once the IP Office receives and enters into the Registry a final and enforceable court decision establishing that the indication is being used as a usual name for a certain type of products.[226]

352. The protection of a registered DO or registered GI shall terminate with the effect *ex tunc* if, upon a substantiated proposal of an interested person, the IP Office cancels the decision on registration of a DO/GI, after it determines that the registration requirements were not met at the time such decision was issued. The party interested in initiating the cancellation proceedings has to submit the evidence supporting the cancellation reasons, as well as to pay the prescribed fee. A proposal for cancellation of registration shall be submitted to the right holder. The latter shall be invited to submit its observations. The IP Office may decide to schedule an oral hearing. The IP Office may decide to cancel the registration of a DO/GI, or to reject the claim. A decision may be appealed before the Government of Serbia within fifteen days from the day of the receipt of such a decision. The Government decision on appeal may be subject to administrative dispute before the Administrative Court. Cancellation of decision to register a DO/GI shall not however affect any court decision related to infringement of rights that is final and enforceable at the time of issuance of such decision, provided that claimant acted in good faith.[227]

224. *Ibid.*, Art. 31.
225. *Ibid.*, Art. 67.
226. *Ibid.*, Art. 68.
227. *Ibid.*, Arts 62–66.

353. Further to the issue of validity of registration of a DO/GI, the status of authorized user has to be renewed under specific rules.[228] Once recognized, the status of authorized user of a DO/GI is valid for three years from the date of entry of the recognition decision in the Registry of authorized users, kept by the IP Office. Such status may be renewed an unlimited number of times, provided the authorized user submits evidence that the requirements prescribed by the law are met and provided that the prescribed fee is paid. The status of authorized user may be renewed only if the registration of a DO/GI is still valid. When requesting the renewal, the applicant has to submit the proof of control of quality and specific characteristics of the product undertaken by an accredited organization. If the IP Office finds that the prescribed requirements are met, it shall enter the decision on renewal into the Registry of authorized users. If not, it shall issue a decision rejecting the request for renewal. Such decision may be appealed before the Government of Serbia within fifteen days from the day of the receipt of such a decision. The Government decision on appeal may be subject to administrative dispute before the Administrative Court.

354. As it may be concluded from the previous explanations, the status of authorized user of a registered DO/GI shall terminate if the user fails to renew its status by not requesting the renewal and/or not paying the prescribed fee and/or no longer meeting the requirements related to the quality of the product or the manner of production. Further to this, the status of authorized user may terminate if the user renounces its status – on the first day following the day of submitting the document of renunciation to the IP Office. The status of authorized user shall also cease on the day of termination of registration of a DO/GI to which it is related. Finally, the status of authorized user shall cease to be valid if the natural or legal person died or terminated, except where such status is transferred to legal successors.[229]

355. The status of authorized user of a registered DO or registered GI shall terminate with the effect *ex tunc* if, upon a substantiated proposal of an interested person, the IP Office cancels the decision on recognition of such status, after it determines that the prescribed requirements were not met at the time the decision was issued.[230] The rules on cancellation of registration of a DO/GI apply *mutatis mutandis* to the procedure of cancellation of status of authorized user of a DO/GI.

§9. Infringement and Remedies

356. Infringements of the exclusive rights on indications of geographical origin are subject to civil and criminal remedies. Both types of remedies are regulated under the Indications of Geographical Origin Act, with the subsidiary application of general rules on civil and criminal procedure, and rules on the assessment of damages.

228. *Ibid.*, Arts 48–51.
229. *Ibid.*, Art. 69.
230. *Ibid.*, Art. 70.

357. Civil remedies normally consist of the indemnification of any damages caused by the infringement of the registered DO/GI.[231] An infringement consists in any unauthorized use of a registered DO/GI or of its imitation by any economic operator. A right owner whose right has been infringed may also seek that the court orders the termination of infringement, that the infringing objects be destroyed or altered, that the tools and equipment used to manufacture infringing objects be subtracted, destroyed or altered, that the information on third parties participating in infringement be supplied, as well as that the judgment determining the infringement be published at the cost of the defendant. If infringement of a registered DO/GI was intentional, the plaintiff may request that the defendant compensate him in the amount of up to triple amount of actual damage and lost profit ('punitive damages'). The infringement proceedings may be initiated within three years following the day the plaintiff has become aware of the infringement and the infringer, but not later than within five years following the day when infringement was committed. The action for infringement of a registered DO/GI may be filed by: any national natural or legal persons who, within a specified geographical area, produce the products that are designated by the name of such geographical area; associations of such persons, chambers of commerce, associations of consumers and state authorities that are, within their regular activities, interested in the protection of indications of geographical origin; foreign natural or legal persons or foreign associations, provided that the indication of geographical origin is recognized in its country of origin, and provided that the right to submit the application in Serbia results from international agreements; authorized users of registered DO/GI; public or state prosecutor.

358. The court may order an interim measure at the request of the person who makes it credible that the registered DO/GI has been infringed, or that such infringement is imminent. The interim measure may consist in the seizure or withdrawal from circulation of the infringing products, as well as means for production of those products, and/or in prohibition of pending activities that infringe or may infringe the registered DO/GI. Further to this, at the request of the person who makes it credible that registered DO/GI has been infringed or may be infringed, or that there is a risk of irreparable damage, as well as that there is reasonable doubt that evidence thereof will be destroyed or that it will be impossible to obtain it at a later time, the court may decide to secure evidence without prior notification or hearing of the person from whom the evidence is to be collected from. The securing of evidence may consist in the inspection of premises, seizure of objects, hearing of witnesses and expert witnesses. Both types of measures may be requested even before filing a complaint, provided that subsequently a complaint is filed within thirty days from the date of rendering the decision on interim measure.

359. Further to civil law remedies, the Indications of Geographical Origin Act lists certain types of conduct that are subject to (pseudo) criminal penalties.[232] Namely, a corporation or any other legal person who violates a protected DO/GI is sanctioned on grounds of corporate offence (in Serbian, *privredni prestup*) by a fine.

231. *Ibid.,* Arts 71–79.
232. *Ibid.,* Arts 80–82.

The violation may consist in unauthorized use of a registered DO or registered GI or of their imitations. A responsible person in a legal entity or a natural person acting independently who is found to infringe a protected indication of geographical origin may also be fined. Finally, a legal person who acts as a representative in the exercising of the rights under the Indications of Geographical Origin Act without a power of attorney is sanctioned on grounds of misdemeanour by a fine. The responsible person in a legal entity and a natural person acting independently may also be fined.

§10. Overlapping and Relation to Other Intellectual Property Rights

360. The protection of a geographical name by specific rules on designations of origin and GIs, laid down by the Indications of Geographical Origin Act, may coexist with trademark protection[233] and protection by unfair competition rules. In practice, it is quite frequent that the same person(s) register a geographical name both as a collective trademark and as a DO/GI.

361. However, it may happen that different persons are entitled to use the same geographical name, one being a trademark owner and the other – holder of a registered DO/GI. The same situation could occur between a user of a personal name and a holder of a registered DO/GI. The Indications of Geographical Origin Act lays down provisions regulating the somewhat complex relationship between indications of geographical origin, on the one hand, and personal names and trademarks, on the other hand.[234] A person using his/her personal name in the course of business activities, or that of his/her predecessor in business, may continue doing so as long as such use does not mislead consumers. Also, the provisions of the Indications of Geographical Origin Act does not influence the registration requirements, validity of registration of right to use trademark identical or similar to a registered GI, if application for registration or registration of such trademark was filed or done in good faith, or if trademark rights were acquired through use in good faith prior to filing an application for GI registration. The provisions of the Indications of Geographical Origin Act does not influence the registration requirements, validity of registration of right to use trademark identical or similar to a GI registered on the level of the European Union, if registration of such trademark was done in good faith, or if trademark rights were acquired through bona fide use prior to registration of GI on the level of the European Union in compliance with EU law.

233. As a collective trademark. *See* Trademark Act, Art. 2.
234. Indications of Geographical Origin Act, Arts 58–59.

Selected Bibliography

§1. Intellectual Property in General

I. Books

Besarović, V.: *Intelektualna svojina,* Pravni fakultet Univerziteta u Beogradu, 2011.

Besarović, V.: *Deregulacija viših oblika privredne saradnje sa inostranstvom,* Zavod za udžbenike i nastavna sredstva, Belgrade, 1990.

Damnjanović, K., Marić V.: *Intelektualna svojina,* Službeni glasnik, Pravni fakultet Univerziteta Union, Belgrade, 2007.

Marković, S., Popović, D.: *Pravo intelektualne svojine,* Pravni fakultet Univerziteta u Beogradu, Belgrade, 2014.

Marković, S.: *Pravo intelektualne svojine i informaciono društvo,* Službeni glasnik, Belgrade 2014.

Popović, D. (ed.): *Intelektualna svojina i Internet: nazivi internet domena, autorska dela, žigom zaštićene oznake,* Pravni fakultet Univerziteta u Beogradu, Belgrade, 2015.

Popović, D.: *Isključiva prava intelektualne svojine i slobodna konkurencija,* Pravni fakultet Univerziteta u Beogradu, Belgrade, 2012.

Radulović, B., Popović, D., Aleksić, D.: *The Economic Contribution of Copyright-Based Industries in Serbia,* World Intellectual Property Organization, Geneva, 2014.

Radišić, J.: *Obligaciono pravo – opšti deo,* Nomos, Belgrade, 2000.

Stanković, O., Vodinelić, V.: *Uvod u građansko pravo,* Nomos, Belgrade, 1996.

Stojanović, Z., Delić, N.: *Krivično pravo – Posebni deo,* Pravni fakultet Univerziteta u Beogradu, Belgrade, 2013.

Žarković, B., Besarović, V.: *Intelektualna svojina: međunarodni ugovori,* Dosije, Belgrade, 2000.

II. Articles

Miladinović Z.: 'Privremene mere i mere obezbeđenja dokaza u slučaju povrede prava intelektualne svojine', in *Pravo i privreda,* n° 4–6/2013, 667–686.

Miladinović, Z.: 'Pravni režim intelektualnih dobara stvorenih u radnom odnosu', in *Pravo i privreda,* n° 7–9/2012, 233–247.

Popović, D.: 'Ugovor o licenci – prilog javnoj raspravi o Prednacrtu Građanskog zakonika Republike Srbije', in *Pravo i privreda,* n° 4–6/2015, 393–411.

Popović, D.: 'Serbian innovation policy as a motor of competitiveness and sustainable development', in E. Alimehmeti ed., *Promotion of scientific research in education,* Centre for SEELS, Skopje, 2014, 89–100.
Popović, D.: 'Kritički osvrt na Sporazum o trgovinskim aspektima prava intelektualne svojine', in V. Radović ed., *Usklađivanje poslovnog prava Srbije sa pravom Evropske unije,* Pravni fakultet Univerziteta u Beogradu, Belgrade, 2011, 357–372.
Popović, D.: 'Teorija neophodnih sredstava: posledice po prava intelektualne svojine', in *Pravo i privreda,* n° 1–4/2008, 126–136.
Radovanović, S.: 'Trostruka naknada u našem pravu intelektualne svojine', in *Pravni život,* n° 11/2003, 829–843.

III. Law Reviews

Business law review. *Pravo i privreda,* Udruženje pravnika u privredi Srbije
General law review. *Anali Pravnog fakulteta u Beogradu,* University of Belgrade – Faculty of Law

§2. Copyright and Neighbouring Rights

I. Books

Marković, S.: *Zaštita računarskih programa patentom, autorskim pravom i pravom sui generis,* Center za mednarodno sodelovanje in razvoj, Ljubljana, 1989.
Marković, S.: *Osnovi autorskog i susednih prava,* Naučna knjiga, Beograd, 1992.
Radovanović, S.: *Ugovor o licenci softvera,* Pravni fakultet Univerziteta u Beogradu, Belgrade 2012.

II. Articles

Marković, S.: 'Televizijsko emitovanje sportskih događaja: pravni aspekti', in *Arhiv za pravne i društvene nauke,* n° 3/2002, 375–410.
Marković, S.: 'Građanskopravni aspekti posete pozorišnoj predstavi', in *Anali Pravnog fakulteta u Beogradu,* n° 1–2/2003, 87–108.
Marković, S.: 'Autorsko ugovorno pravo – kreativnost na tržištu', in *Zbornik radova Fakulteta dramskih umetnosti u Beogradu,* n° 11–12/2007, 359–392.
Miladinović, Z., Varga, S: 'Pravo autora na raskid ugovora zbog nevršenja ustupljenih ovlašćenja', in *Pravo i privreda,* n° 4–6/2011, 882–897.
Miladinović, Z.: 'Raskid autorskog ugovora zbog promenjenih shvatanja autora (pravo pokajanja)', in *Pravo i privreda,* n° 5–8/2009, 13–24.
Miladinović, Z.: 'Suspenzija isključivih imovinskopravnih ovlašćenja autora', in *Pravo i privreda,* n° 5–8/2005, 645–658.
Popović, D.: 'Kritički osvrt na srodnopravnu zaštitu izdavača: zaštita privrednog ili kulturnog poduhvata', in *Anali Pravnog fakulteta u Beogradu,* n° 1/2015, 116–132.
Popović, D.: 'O ograničenjima i kolektivnom ostvarivanju autorskog prava i srodnih prava', in *Pravo i privreda,* n° 7–9/2012, 294–317.
Popović, D.: 'Povreda autorskog prava i srodnih prava na sajtovima za razmenu audio i video zapisa, putem korišćenja onlajn video igara i na blogovima', in *Pravni život,* n° 11/2012, 789–804.

Popović, D.: 'Povreda autorskog prava i srodnih prava na Internetu: preispitivanje uloge posrednika', in *Pravo i privreda,* n° 4–6/2010, 579–593.

Radovanović, S.: 'Može li autorsko imovinsko pravo da bude predmet zalaganja?', in *Pravo i privreda,* n° 7–9/2014, 37–54.

Radovanović, S.: 'Zastarelost potraživanja naknada organizacija za kolektivno ostvarivanje autorskog i srodnih prava', in *Zbornik radova Pravnog fakulteta u Novom Sadu,* n° 4/2014, 265–277.

Radovanović, S.: 'Neka pitanja u vezi sa naplatom posebne naknade u slučaju umnožavanja za privatne potrebe', in B. Vlašković ed., *Pravne i infrastrukturne osnove za razvoj ekonomije zasnovane na znanju (2013),* Pravni fakultet Univerziteta u Kragujevcu, Kragujevac, 2013, 175–189.

Radovanović, S.: 'Obim dozvoljenog umnožavanja računarskog programa kod ugovora o licenci', in *Anali Pravnog fakulteta u Beogradu,* n° 1/2013, 169–197.

Radovanović, S.: 'Tehnološke mere u sistemu zaštite autorskog prava', in *Zbornik radova Pravnog fakulteta u Novom Sadu,* n° 1/2011, 399–411.

Radovanović, S.: 'Neka pitanja u vezi sa naknadom štete u autorskom pravu', in *Pravni život,* n° 11/2002, 1071–1083.

§3. Patents

I. Books

Janjić, M.: *Ugovori o licenci (posebno međunarodni ugovori o licenci),* Institut za uporedno pravo, Belgrade, 1967.

Marković, S.: *Patentno pravo,* Nomos, Belgrade, 1997.

Vlašković, B.: *Sadržina i povreda patenta,* Pravni fakultet Univerziteta u Kragujevcu, Kragujevac, 1999.

II. Articles

Marković, S.: 'Pravo ranijeg korisnika patentiranog pronalaska kao ograničenje patenta: ogled o jednom marginalnom pitanju patentnog prava', in *Pravo i privreda,* n° 7–9/2014, 13–27.

Marković, S.: 'Globalna administrativna kriza patentnog sistema', in *Anali Pravnog fakulteta u Beogradu,* n° 2/2006, 93–121.

Popović, D.: 'Usklađivanje patentnog prava Republike Srbije sa međunarodnopravnim standardima zaštite pronalazaka', in V. Radović ed., *Usklađivanje poslovnog prava Srbije sa pravom Evropske unije (2012),* Pravni fakultet Univerziteta u Beogradu, Beograd, 2012, 281–303.

Radovanović, S.: 'Patenti i javno zdravlje – prinudna licenca za izvoz farmaceutskih proizvoda', in *Pravo i privreda,* n° 4–6/2013, 744–762.

Radovanović, S.: 'Načini i pravne posledice prestanka ugovora o licenci', in *Pravo i privreda,* n° 7–9/2012, 338–356.

Varga, S., Planojević, N.: 'Prevencija rizika po realizaciju založnog prava na patentu', in B. Vlašković ed., *Pravne i infrastrukturne osnove za razvoj ekonomije zasnovane na znanju (2012),* Pravni fakultet Univerziteta u Kragujevcu, Kragujevac, 2012, 397–413.

Varga, S.: 'Ograničenja patenta', in *Pravo i privreda,* n° 5–8/2009, 66–80.

Vlašković, B.: 'Apsolutno dejstvo patenta u vezi sa pronalascima sekvenci gena', in *Pravo i privreda,* n° 7–9/2012, 218–233.

§4. Petty Patents

I. Books

Marković, S.: *Patentno pravo,* Nomos, Belgrade, 1997.

II. Articles

Marković, S.: 'Mali patent u patentnom pravu Srbije', in B. Vlašković ed., *Pravne i infrastrukturne osnove za razvoj ekonomije zasnovane na znanju (2013),* Pravni fakultet Univerziteta u Kragujevcu, Kragujevac, 2013, 65–77.

Varga, S.: 'Intelektualne tvorevine koje se ne smatraju pronalascima', in *Pravo i privreda,* n° 4–6/2010, 594–606.

§5. Trademarks

I. Books

Marić, V.: *Sličnost žigova,* Pravni fakultet Univerziteta Union, Belgrade, 2009.

Popović, D.: *Registracija naziva internet domena i pravo žiga,* Pravni fakultet Univerziteta u Beogradu, 2014.

Vlašković, B.: *Deskriptivni znaci u pravu o žigovima,* Prizma, Kragujevac, 1996.

Vlašković, B.: *Pravna zaštita slavnih žigova,* Savezni zavod za patente, Belgrade, 1992.

II. Articles

Marković, S.: 'Roba u tranzitu i zaštita prava intelektualne svojine u carinskom postupku', in B. Vlašković ed., *Pravne i infrastrukturne osnove za razvoj ekonomije zasnovane na znanju (2012),* Pravni fakultet Univerziteta u Kragujevcu, Kragujevac, 2012, 151–165.

Popović, D.: 'Harmonizacija pravila o zaštiti znakova razlikovanja u svetlu pristupanja Srbije Singapurskom ugovoru o žigovnom pravu', in V. Radović ed., *Usklađivanje poslovnog prava Srbije sa pravom Evropske unije (2013),* Pravni fakultet Univerziteta u Beogradu, Beograd, 2013, 177–197.

Popović, D.: 'Žigom zaštićene oznake, ključne reči i oglašavanje na Internetu', in *Pravo i privreda,* n° 4–6/2011, 927–947.

Spasojević, S.: 'Prestanak žiga zbog nekorišćenja', in *Pravo i privreda,* n° 4–6/2011, 964–974.

Spasojević, S.: 'Kvar ili promena stanja žigom označene robe posle njenog prvog stavljanja u promet', in *Pravo i privreda,* n° 5–8/2009, 106–117.

Vlašković, B.: 'Trodimenzionalni znakovi koji nisu podesni za zaštitu žigom', in B. Vlašković ed., *Pravne i infrastrukturne osnove za razvoj ekonomije zasnovane na znanju (2013),* Pravni fakultet Univerziteta u Kragujevcu, Kragujevac, 2013, 77–89.

Vlašković, B.: 'Distinktivnost kao uslov za registraciju žiga', in *Pravo i privreda,* n° 7–9/2015, 11–21.

§6. Tradenames

I. Books

Vasiljević, M.: *Trgovinsko pravo,* Pravni fakultet Univerziteta u Beogradu, Belgrade, 2012.
Vasiljević, M.: *Kompanijsko pravo,* Pravni fakultet Univerziteta u Beogradu, Belgrade, 2012.

II. Articles

Marković, S.: 'Zaštita i pravna priroda firme', in *Pravo i privreda,* n° 3–6/1995, 551–561.

§7. Industrial Designs

I. Articles

Vlašković, B.: 'Obim zaštite žiga i prava na industrijski dizajn, i njihova kolizija', in M. Mićović ed., *Dvadeset prvi vek – vek usluga i uslužnog prava (knjiga druga),* Pravni fakultet Univerziteta u Kragujevcu, Kragujevac, 2011, 215–232.

§8. Plant Varieties

I. Articles

Marković, S.: 'Pravna zaštita novih biljnih sorti', in *Glasnik Pravnog fakulteta u Kragujevcu,* 1982, 105–125.
Marković, S.: 'Harmonizacija jugoslovenskog prava sortne zaštite sa evropskom i drugom međunarodnom regulativom', in *Pravni život,* n° 11/1997, 753–764.
Spasić, V.: 'Nova legislativa o pravu oplemenjivača biljnih sorti u Srbiji', in *Anali Pravnog fakulteta u Beogradu,* n° 7–9/2012, 279–294.

§9. Topographies of Semiconducting Products

I. Articles

Miladinović, Z.: 'Sadržina i zaštita prava na topografiju integrisanih kola', in *Pravo i privreda,* n° 5–8/2004, 998–1010.

§10. Trade Secrets

I. Books

Zabel, B., Pretnar, S.: *Poslovna tajna,* Institut za uporedno pravo, Belgrade, 1970.

II. Articles

Marković, S.: 'Poslovna tajna kao predmet ugovora o prenosu industrijske svojine', in *Pravni život,* n° 11–12/1993, 1631–1648.

Selected Bibliography

§11. Indications of Geographical Origin

I. Articles

Popović, D.: 'Oznake geografskog porekla i generični nazivi', in *Pravo i privreda,* n° 5–8/2007, 648–657.

Remović, B.: 'OGP proizvodi u Srbiji – izazovi sertifikacije', in B. Vlašković ed., *Pravne i infrastrukturne osnove za razvoj ekonomije zasnovane na znanju (2013),* Pravni fakultet Univerziteta u Kragujevcu, Kragujevac, 2013, 251–269.

Spasojević, S.: 'Ekonomski značaj oznaka geografskog porekla i tipični oblici njihove zloupotrebe', in B. Vlašković ed., *Pravne i infrastrukturne osnove za razvoj ekonomije zasnovane na znanju (2012),* Pravni fakultet Univerziteta u Kragujevcu, Kragujevac, 2012, 315–327.

Živojinović, D., Varga, S.: 'Prenos ovlašćenja na korišćenje oznake geografskog porekla mortis causa', in B. Vlašković ed., *Pravne i infrastrukturne osnove za razvoj ekonomije zasnovane na znanju (2012),* Pravni fakultet Univerziteta u Kragujevcu, Kragujevac, 2012, 243–257.

Index

The numbers here refer to paragraph numbers.

Index